INTERPRETING LUKE - ACTS
FOR THE LOCAL CHURCH

Luke Speaks For Himself

Paul L. Hammer

MELLEN BIBLICAL PRESS
Lewiston/Queenston/Lampeter

Library of Congress Cataloging-in-Publication Data

Hammer, Paul L.
   Interpreting Luke-Acts for the local church : Luke speaks for
himself / Paul L. Hammer.
      p.   cm.
   Includes bibliographical references and index.
   ISBN 0-7734-2388-5
   1. Bible. N.T. Luke--Criticism, interpretation, etc. 2. Bible.
N.T. Acts--Criticism, interpretation, etc.   I. Title.
BS2589.H34   1994
226.4'06--dc20   93-40594
                                                                      CIP

A CIP catalog record for this book is available from the British Library.

All rights reserved. For information contact

The Edwin Mellen Press   The Edwin Mellen Press
        Box 450   Box 67
Lewiston, New York   Queenston,Ontario
     USA 14092   CANADA L0S 1L0

The Edwin Mellen Press, Ltd.
Lampeter, Dyfed, Wales
UNITED KINGDOM   SA48 7DY

Printed in the United States of America

To Esther in deepest gratitude and joy

for 40 years of sharing together

Contents

Power for mission among Jews

Power for mission among Samaritans

Power for mission among Gentiles

A final note on Paul and the Spirit

God's reign in Jesus in the present

God's reign in the future

Eating and drinking in the future

Preaching and praying for God's reign

Giving priority to God's reign

What kind of a king

Salvation, savior, save

Joy, rejoice

Repentance and forgiveness

Prayer

Table

Solidarity with Israel

The disciples of Jesus in *Luke*

The community in *Acts*

Marks of the community in *Acts*

    Witness

    Learning and worship

    Healing

    Confrontation

Preface

I have written this book in the first person as if I were Luke himself. I sought to let him interpret his Gospel of Luke and The Acts of the Apostles. This made the writing very alive, both for me and for the two groups mentioned below. I have tried to be faithful both to the text of *Luke-Acts* and to Lukan scholars, though at points I have risked the fun of suggesting some possibilities beyond full evidence in *Luke-Acts*.

I enlisted the participation of two different groups to provide regular feedback and input. One was African-American inner city pastors and laity from western New York who participate in our seminary's Program of Education and Action for Responsible Leadership. The other was people in a suburban congregation where I am a member. I presented a chapter a week for ten weeks to each group. Their participation and response as interpreting communities helped to test out my goal and contribute to the final product. I am deeply grateful to them for their excitement, encouragement, and enrichment.

I also want to thank my spouse Esther for her very perceptive reading and critique of the manuscript and her valuable suggestions for enhancing its clarity at many points. Further, my gratitude goes to my New Testament colleagues and friends, Charles Talbert and Paul Achtemeier, for their very helpful comments.

In quoting from *Luke-Acts* I have used the New Revised Standard Version. In the Endnotes I do not speak in the first person as "Luke" but make my own comments and references. Though I am gratefully dependent in part on the scholarly works that I have read, digested, and taught over the years, it is not my primary purpose in this book to engage or report them. I do hope that my list for further reading at the end may prove useful for those who may want to pursue further study.

What I have written is not a verse by verse or chapter by chapter commentary. Rather I intend to provide some overall understanding that will help readers gain a perspective for interpreting *Luke-Acts* and a feel for this very important New Testament writer. Since materials in various chapters do overlap at points, the reader should not be surprised if some texts and themes from *Luke-Acts* appear more than once.

Many people see a gap in biblical understanding between students in a seminary or university and people in local churches. As a New Testament seminary teacher, I would like to help overcome that gap by presenting scholarly perspectives on *The Gospel of Luke* and *The Acts of the Apostles* as simply as possible. My primary audience is people in local churches who want to gain an informed understanding of these writings in language they can understand. It also may prove useful to seminary students and pastors as well.

I hope that what I have written will help to further "the good news of great joy for all the people."

Paul L. Hammer
Professor of New Testament Interpretation
Colgate Rochester/Bexley Hall/Crozer Divinity School
Rochester, New York

Introduction

"Do not be afraid; for see - I am bringing you good news of great joy for all the people" (Lk. 2:10).

Sisters and brothers, I pray that God's peace and joy will be yours as I speak with you now some 1900 years after I wrote *Luke-Acts*. I had no idea then that my writings would become part of your Bibles and comprise a fourth of what you call the New Testament. Our Bible was the Hebrew Scriptures - what you call the Old Testament. However, since many of us did not know Hebrew, we read it in a Greek translation and wrote in Greek ourselves. This was because, four centuries earlier, Alexander the Great had spread Greek language and culture throughout the eastern Mediterranean world, and Greek became the major language.

I never identify or speak about myself in my writings - others gave titles to them later,[1] but here let me say that I learned about both Greek culture and the Hebrew heritage of Israel. I had friends from both Jewish and Gentile backgrounds and could appreciate that Timothy had a Jewish mother and a Greek father (Acts 16:1). I suppose that is part of the reason my writings sought to break down barriers between Jews and Gentiles and among all people. Jesus was and is "good news of great joy for *all* people."

I wrote *Luke-Acts* about 60 years after Jesus' death and resurrection - after the destruction of Jerusalem by the Romans in 70 C.E. and before Christian persecution by the Emperor Domitian in the 90's. I had hoped that my writings, addressed to Theophilus (Lk. 1:3; Acts 1:1) - to "God-lover" and all God-lovers - would have helped to divert such persecution. I wanted the Christian witness to go on with unhindered boldness (Acts 28:31).

That partly explains why I wrote my stories of Jesus and the early church. I wanted to interpret them and write a compelling picture of God's Spirit in Jesus and the church at work for peace on earth (Lk. 2:14; Acts 10:36). Though what I wrote in *Luke-Acts* is rooted in history, I was no simple chronicler of events. I shaped and reshaped the stories to interpret and proclaim their larger meaning for my time. I wanted to help further the Christian mission then "to the ends of the earth" (Acts 1:8).

The chapters that follow are to complement the reading of *Luke* and *Acts* themselves. I hope the chapters of my book will be more like useful footnotes. What I wrote in *Luke-Acts* is the message that has become part of the church's scripture through the centuries - to guide and nourish and challenge the readers.

When you read them, do so out loud. Such oral communication was the major method in my time. This lets you see and hear and taste the text for a triple impact on your mind and heart. Hopefully, as you interpret them for your time, you will respond like the two Emmaus road disciples did to Jesus' interpretation of the Hebrew scriptures: "Were not our hearts burning within us. . .while he was opening the scriptures to us?" (Lk. 24:32).

Endnotes

[1]Though later tradition developed to make Luke, a physician, the writer, there is no evidence in *Luke-Acts* to support this. People linked such writings to certain names in order to connect them to major authoritative persons, in Luke's instance to Paul (see Philem. 24; Col. 4:14; 2 Tim. 4:11).

CHAPTER 1

Why I Wrote Luke-Acts

"so that you may know the truth (Lk. 1:4)

To extend the witness

I wrote first to help extend the witness to God's healing deed in Jesus throughout the Roman Empire. I wanted to follow through in my time on Jesus' words to his first disciples:[1]

"You are witnesses of these things" (Lk. 24:48).

"You shall be my witnesses in Jerusalem and in all Judea and Samaria and to the end of the earth" (Acts 1:8).

I did not want any misunderstanding of Jesus and the church to get in the way of our testimony, a testimony that really was and is "good news of great joy for all the people" (Lk. 2:10).

As I show at the beginning of *Luke* (1:1-4), though indebted to others, I could not simply repeat what they already had done. My time and my community called for a fresh reshaping of the story to dispel distorted understandings and make valuable additions. When I wrote, "so that you may know the truth," I did not mean simply getting the facts straight. I meant getting the *meaning* of Jesus'

life and ministry, death and resurrection, exaltation and reign, clear for the sake
of witnessing to the good news.

To meet political concerns

I wrote after the Romans crushed the Jewish uprising and destroyed
Jerusalem in 70 C.E., and I weave my knowledge of what happened into Jesus'
prophetic words about this (Lk. 21:20-24). I did not want to see Jesus and early
Christians understood as military insurrectionists. To see them in this way would
provide a reason for crushing Christians in my time.

Jesus was a revolutionary and Christians "have been turning the world
upside down" (Acts 17:6), but they did not seek military conquest. When Peter
declares Jesus as the Messiah, the Christ, God's "anointed," Jesus interprets it in
terms of suffering. He challenged the popular understanding of the Messiah as one
to crush the Romans with political and military power (Lk. 9:18-22).

As a revolutionary, Jesus did want to turn the world upside down, but to
bring life, not death; joy, not sorrow; hope, not despair; love, not hate; peace, not
war. He wanted to lift people up and include them in God's one human family,
not put them down and exclude them.

I wanted to help create a political climate in the Empire which allowed a
"proclaiming the kingdom of God and teaching about the Lord Jesus Christ *with
all boldness and without hindrance.*" I ended my entire two-part work with those
words and in that spirit of freedom to speak (Acts 28:31).

Memories of Nero Caesar's persecuting Christians in Rome, and of
Christians caught up in the Roman destruction of Jerusalem, understandably
caused hostility of Christians toward Rome and suspicion of Romans toward
Christians. I wanted to promote a favorable relationship between them for the sake
of bold and unhindered witness to the good news in Jesus.

I did make a point of putting some Romans in a good light. Jews told of
a Roman soldier (centurion) "who loves our people, and it is he who built our
synagogue for us," and Jesus praised his faith (Lk. 7:1-10). The Roman soldier

Cornelius was an "upright and God-fearing man, who is well spoken of by the whole Jewish nation" (Acts 10:22; note also 10:2).

Though he finally succumbed and agreed to put Jesus to death, the Roman Pilate declared Jesus innocent of any crime against Rome three times (Lk. 23:4,14,22), and a Roman soldier at the foot of the cross said of Jesus, "Certainly this man was innocent (Lk. 23:47).

I tell how Paul's being a Roman citizen helped him when he had been beaten and jailed (Acts 16:35-39), and the Roman Gallio declared him innocent of any "crime or serious villainy (Acts 18:12-17; see also 23:26-30). A Roman tribune and Roman soldiers kept Paul from beating and death (Acts 21:30-33), and his Roman citizenship saved him from further flogging (Acts 22:25-29).

Though he was in custody, the Roman provincial governor treated Paul well (Acts 24:22-23), and his successor and others said of Paul, "This man is doing nothing to deserve death or imprisonment" (Acts 26:30-31). The local king said of Paul, "This man could have been set free if he had not appealed to the Emperor" (Acts 26:32; see also 28:17-19). On the sea journey to Rome, a Roman officer saved Paul from being killed (Acts 27:42-44).

Though he is under house arrest, I concluded *Acts* with Paul free (as I quoted earlier) for "proclaiming the kingdom of God and teaching about the Lord Jesus Christ with all boldness and without hindrance." I was convinced that this more favorable view of Romans would help to support such bold and unhindered witness.

Yet, Paul finally was put to death in Rome.[2] Since I wrote *Acts* more than twenty years later and knew of Paul's death, why didn't I tell of it? Well, if I wanted to help create a good climate for spreading the good news throughout the Empire in my time, would rubbing salt in the old sores of Paul's death at the hands of the Romans help? It would only impede it. I chose to leave a picture of Paul's bold and unhindered preaching and teaching to inspire folks for the same in my time.

To respond to a continuing history

People in my time had to face the fact that the final coming of Jesus and the fullness of God's reign, expected by first generation Christians in their lifetime, did not occur. My readers and I were second or third generation Christians. What were we to do with such disappointed expectations? When is Jesus coming? Why is history continuing?

The fact that I wrote *Acts* is part of my answer. Why a continuing history? Because it provides an opportunity to continue the spread of the good news "to the end of the earth." We were not to sit around and wait for the end. Now Jesus was sending us as witnesses in our time. People in *Acts* began the witness. We were to continue it.

We did not give up on Jesus' final coming, but we did release it from any timetable. I was partly dependent on those who preceded me (see Lk. 1:1-2). At points I reflect their expectation of the nearness of Jesus' final coming and the end of history, but I finally had to challenge their view.

I knew and used the *Gospel of Mark* (more on this in chapter 2). In *Mark* Jesus first "sermon" reads, "The time is fulfilled, and the kingdom of God has come near; repent and believe in the good news" (Mk. 1:15). A marvelous message! Why did I choose not to include it near the beginning of *Luke*?

I saw the possibility of people interpreting it as still proclaiming the nearness of the end. Some 60 years after Jesus' ministry, I did not want to promote further any such disappointed expectation. So instead of Mark's first sermon of Jesus, I tell of Jesus proclaiming the program of his mission by reading from the prophet Isaiah: "good news to the poor . . . release to the captives . . . sight to the blind . . . to let the oppressed go free, to proclaim the year of the Lord's favor" (Lk. 4:18-19).

Luke unfolds that mission of Jesus, but it also pictures the program of the church's mission in a continuing history as reflected in *Acts*. And decades later in my time, it also became a program for our mission.

I did not want my readers to expect that the end was near. I bring Jesus' words to warn them.

> "Beware that you are not led astray; for many will come in my name and
> say, 'I am he!' and 'The time is near!' Do not go after them" (Lk. 21:8).

Rather, I wanted them to take up Jesus' mission in our continuing history. It was a mission of good news and release, of sight and freedom, of peace and joy for all people. God's reign in Jesus was not only something to expect to come in the future. It was and is a reign for us to live and witness to already in the present.

To explain John the Baptist

Some people in my time still believed John the Baptist to be the Messiah, the Christ. John does have an important role in all four gospels as the voice of one crying in the wilderness to prepare the way of the Lord (Lk. 3:4; from Is. 60:3). But for all, Jesus, never John, is the Messiah.

However, apparently John himself had some doubts about Jesus. He sent his disciples to ask Jesus, "Are you he who is to come, or are we to wait for another?" (Lk. 7:18-20). Jesus answers,

> "Go and tell John what you have seen and heard: the blind receive their
> sight, the lame walk, the lepers are cleansed, the deaf hear, the dead are
> raised, the poor have good news brought to them. And blessed is anyone
> who takes no offense at me" (Lk. 7:22-23).

Jesus' deeds showed that he is the one. But then Jesus goes on to affirm John as a prophet and more (Lk. 7:27-28).

I had to make very clear in my time that John's identity was in no way to be confused with Jesus as the Messiah, nor was Jesus in any way dependent on John. I did not even present Jesus as baptized by John. When Jesus is baptized, John already is in prison (see Lk. 3:18-21). I let John speak for himself about his relationship to Jesus.

> "As the people were filled with expectation, and all were questioning in
> their hearts concerning John, whether he might be the Messiah, John

answered them by saying, 'I baptize you with water; but one more powerful than is coming'" (Lk. 3:15-16).

Even the Infancy Stories (Lk. 1-2) raise the issue of John's relationship to Jesus and push it back into the prenatal period. The Infancy Stories devote a major part to John the Baptist. Yet they powerfully portray that he is subordinate to Jesus.

When Mary, pregnant with Jesus, goes to visit Elizabeth, pregnant with John, the child John leaps in the womb for joy at the present of Jesus in Mary's womb (Lk. 1:39-44). In the story, even before they are born, John expresses his joy and subordination to Jesus. I wanted such a story to help answer the question of John's identity. His role is highly significant as a witness to the Messiah, but none are to see him as the Messiah himself.

To interpret the Good News

I was an interpreter of Jesus and the early church. I had to tell the story for my time and my community, first of God's Spirit at work in Jesus (in *Luke*) and then of God's Spirit at work in the first generation of Christians (in *Acts*). I saw Jesus and the first Christians as the foundation for calling my readers of the second and third generation to continue Jesus' mission of good news.

My task was to update the past for the present - to interpret the past of Jesus and the earliest Christians in ways that would meet the mission needs of my community in the present. In reading *Luke-Acts*, this means to read them not so much as a source of *factual* history but as *interpreted* history. I was not so much a reporter as a story teller, though my stories are rooted in Jesus and the early church. The facts of the past have become stories for the present to nourish and guide and challenge people with good news. This updating, interpreting work I understand as part of the ongoing work of God's Holy Spirit.

The work of the Spirit is not locked in the past in Jesus or the early church. That Spirit continued to work in my time. I wanted to let the Spirit work in my retelling the story for my community. I wanted to tell not only who Jesus was but who he is; not only what he did but what he is doing; not only what he said but what he is saying as our risen Lord. My writing sought to serve to proclaim Jesus as Good News in the present.

I never used the noun "gospel" (*euangelion*, "good news"), but I used the verb "to-preach-the-gospel" (*euangelizesthai*) more than 25 times.[3] You derive your English word "evangelical" directly from that Greek word. All Christians are evangelicals, for we all have our life in God's evangel, God's good news in Jesus. I used the verb form because verbs are action words, and the good news calls for active proclamation.

For me, this evangelical, "good news" witness intended to break down all human barriers throughout the Empire: the barriers of nation and language, gender and race, religion and social class.[4] It is ecumenical (for the whole "inhabited world") and reaches out to all people.

I take my genealogy of Jesus (Lk. 3:23-28) back to "Adam" - to the Hebrew word that means "humanity." Jesus is the heir of the whole human race. He belongs to everyone.

You can see something of my evangelical and ecumenical concern by noting the great diversity of peoples in *Luke-Acts*: parents, children, wives, husbands, mixed marriages, brothers, sisters; young women, young men, old men, old women, widows, eunuchs; slaves, freed, masters, servants, rich, poor; educated, uneducated, in-groups, outcasts, circumcised, uncircumcised; sick, persons with disabilities, demon-possessed, dead.

There are more: fishermen, business women, business men, beggars, prostitutes; tax collectors, judges, jailers, prisoners; officers, soldiers, police, politicians (emperors, kings, tetrarchs, governors, tribunes, proconsuls, local magistrates, island chiefs).

There are still more: teachers, preachers, prophets, martyrs, philosophers, theologians, lawyers; magicians, devotees of mystery religions, temple priests, synagogue rulers; traitors, revolutionaries, liars, truth-tellers; Syrians, Ethiopians,

Greeks, Romans, Jews, Samaritans. I wanted to include them all as objects of God's good news.

Earliest Christians had their problems, but I did not choose to rehearse them decades later. To rub salt in old sores of struggle and disunity would gain nothing for the mission in my time. I chose rather to show how they worked out their problems (see Acts 15) for the sake of a united witness across human barriers.

I let Peter's words in *Acts* express much of my view:

"I truly understand that God shows no partiality, but in every nation anyone who fears God and does what is right is acceptable to God. You know the message God sent to the people of Israel, preaching peace by Jesus Christ - he is Lord of all" (Acts 10:36).

So I wrote for my own Christian community to encourage further their witness in the Empire. But I wrote also for those beyond the church who needed to know that Jesus Christ was not their enemy. He was "good news of great joy for all people."

With these reasons for writing *Luke-Acts*, what were the sources for what I wrote? I will discuss that in our next conversation.

Endnotes

[1]The "witness" word family (*marturein, marturia, martus*) occurs more than 30 times in *Luke-Acts*: Lk. 4:22 ("spoke well of"); Acts 1:22; 2:32; 3:15; 5:32; 10:39,41,43; 13:31; 14:3; 15:8; 22:15; 23:11; 26:16,22.

[2]Tradition has it that Paul was martyred in Rome in the reign of Nero Caesar. A few scholars want to date the writing of *Acts* earlier and maintain that *Acts* does not tell of Paul's death because the writer didn't know of it.

[3]Angels (God's messengers) bring the gospel (Lk. 1:19; 2:10); John the Baptist proclaims good news (Lk. 3:18); Jesus brings good news (Lk. 4:18,43; 7:22; 8:1); the disciples bring good news (Lk. 9:6; see also 16:16); in *Acts* the church's witness proclaims good news again and again (Acts 5:42; 8:4,12,25,35, 40; 10:36; 11:20; 13:32; 14:7,15,21; 15:35; 16:10; 17:18).

[4]The word *oikoumene* ("inhabited world") occurs several times in *Luke-Acts*: Lk. 2:1; 4:5; 21:26; Acts 11:28; 17:6,31; 19:27; 24:5.

CHAPTER 2

Sources of My Materials

"Since many have undertaken to set down an orderly account of the events that have been fulfilled among us, just as they were handed on to us by those who from the beginning were eyewitnesses and servants of the word, I too decided . . . to write" (Lk. 1:1-2)

My friends

I had the benefit of living in a setting that acquainted me with Jewish customs and scripture, as well as with Greek culture and literature. Among my friends and acquaintences were persons of both Jewish and gentile backgrounds.[1]

Some believed in Jesus as the Messiah and helped me to see how important Israel's heritage and scripture were to understand Jesus as good news for both Jews and Gentiles. They shared the spirit of Jesus' Jewish mother:

"My soul magnifies the Lord, and my spirit rejoices in God my Savior"
(Lk. 1:47).

They knew how to treasure the words of good news and ponder them in their hearts (Lk. 2:19).

Other acquaintences were similar to what I wrote about the Gentile Cornelius: "a devout man who feared God with all his household; he gave alms generously to the people and prayed constantly to God" (Acts 10:2). Like

Cornelius, they had come to experience that "the gift of the Holy Spirit had been poured out even on the Gentiles" (Acts 10:45).

So some shared with me aspects of their Hebrew heritage, others aspects of their Greek heritage. I reflect the latter in my story of Paul's visit to Athens in his references to Epicurean and Stoic philosophers and Greek poets (Acts 17:18,28).

My writing of *Luke-Acts* expressed not only my theological conviction about the link between Jews and Gentiles. It expressed also the personal link between my Jewish and Gentile friends who were part of the source of my theological conviction. Jesus was and is good news for both Jews and Gentiles. Simeon expressed this in prayer as he saw the infant Jesus:

> "my eyes have seen your salvation, which you have prepared in the presence of all peoples, a light for revelation to *the Gentiles* and for glory to your *people Israel*" (Lk. 2:30-32).

My church community

My participation in a church community of both Jewish and Gentile Christians expanded their influence. In that community I learned further how important the Hebrew heritage was for both Jews and Gentiles.

Jesus himself was Jewish, and all of the *first* followers of Jesus were Jews. I emphasized this connection to the Jewish community in *Luke-Acts*.[2] Some people even saw Jesus' followers simply as another Jewish sect.

Paul never saw himself other than as a Jew, but a Jew whose encounter with the risen Lord transformed his life from persecutor to proclaimer of Jesus as the Jewish Messiah.[3] It is striking that the *Jewish* Paul became the most important missionary to *Gentiles*. The roots of the Gentile mission are in the community of Israel. Paul even explains the *Christian* mission with words from Israel's prophet Isaiah:

> "I have set you to be a light for the Gentiles, so that you may bring salvation to the ends of the earth" (Acts 13:47, from Is. 49:6).

Yet, even though their roots joined them together, by my time the lines between official Judaism and the church had hardened.[4] Official Judaism simply could not accept a *crucified* messiah. The break was especially painful for families like mine with personal ties to Israel. Sometimes synagogue leaders persecuted members of my church community. Jesus' prophetic words became very real (see Lk. 12:11; 21:12).

Still, we patterned our worship on the synagogue service: hymns and scripture readings, teaching and prayer. We also would "break bread" with our risen Lord (note Lk. 24:30). My words about the church in Acts fitted my community quite well.

> "They devoted themselves to the apostles' teaching and fellowship, to the
> breaking of bread and the prayers" (Acts 2:42).

We also tried to meet one another's economic needs. We praised God. We promoted good will among us (see Acts 2:44-47).

The life of my community contributed directly to my writing. I wove hymns we sang into the Infancy Stories.[5] I included prayers we prayed[6] and texts we treasured from our Hebrew scriptures.[7] Jesus' parables made us think and challenged us to change our lives.[8] Stories of Jesus' ministry lifted our horizons.[9]

Some materials lived orally in our worship and witness before we ever wrote them down. Some of them found their way into *Luke-Acts*.[10] To write them down in my time meant that we could preserve hymns and prayers, parables and stories, used orally by earlier Christians. We could help let them live on.

I was not a writer, inspired by the Spirit all by myself. I was a member of an inspired community. The Holy Spirit was at work among us as we worked and worshiped and witnessed to interpret the good news together in our time. Life in my church community was indispensable in my writing *Luke-Acts*.

The Gospel of Mark

I noted earlier that I knew *The Gospel of Mark*. It is one of the writings to which I refer at the beginning of *Luke* (Lk. 1:1). "Mark"[11] wrote about 70

C.E., nearly two decades before I did. He compiled and shaped stories of Jesus' ministry, suffering, death, and resurrection. These had been circulating largely in oral forms in the preaching, teaching, and mission outreach of the first generation of Christians.

Forty years after Jesus' death and resurrection, most eyewitnesses to Jesus' ministry were gone. The need arose to preserve materials in writing and shape them to meet the needs of new situations. This is true especially if Christians no longer expected Jesus' final coming and history's end soon. Their lives had to continue and written materials would help their witness.

Mark's community lived on the edge between the first and second generation of Christians and may still have maintained that near expectation of the end. They knew persecution (see Mk. 10:30; 13:9-13) and Mark wrote, "if the Lord had not cut short those days, no one would be saved" (Mk. 13:20).

Yet the timing of the end remained a question. As Mark told the story, not even Jesus knew when, only the Father (Mk. 13:32). Did Mark suggest to his community that, if Jesus didn't know the time, they should not try to set a time either? Two decades after Mark wrote for his community, we certainly no longer tried to set any such time. In my use of Mark, I omit any reference to the verses from Mark cited above (Mk. 13:20, 32).

I derived about a third of *Luke* from *The Gospel of Mark* and construct what I wrote along Markan lines, though I omit one major section and insert many other materials.[12] Also, whereas Mark begins the story of Jesus with his baptism, I begin with the Infancy Stories (Lk. 1-2) and take the story back to his birth. Further, whereas Mark has no resurrection appearances of Jesus,[13] I do (Lk. 24:13-52). Then too I have the whole second half of my two-part work, *The Acts of the Apostles*.

In my use of *The Gospel of Mark*, I adapted and reshaped parts of it to meet the needs of my community in a later setting. If you compare similar texts in *Mark* and *Luke*, you readily can see where I add, omit, or make a new emphasis.[14] Let me illustrate. Read and compare *Mark* and *Luke* below. Then note my comments.

An example of a "gospel parallels"

The beginning of the Gospel of Jesus Christ, the Son of God.

In the fifteenth year of the reign of Emperor Tiberius when Pontius Pilate was governor of Judea. . . 2 during the priesthood of Annas and Caiaphas, the word of God came to John son of Zechariah in the wilderness. 3 He went into all the region around the Jordan, proclaiming a baptism of repentance for the for as it is written in the book of the prophet Isaiah,

2 As it is written in the prophet Isaiah, "See I am sending my messenger ahead of you, who will prepare your way; 3 the voice of one crying out in the wilderness; 'Prepare the way of the Lord, make his paths straight.'" 4 John the baptizer appeared in the wilderness, proclaiming a baptism of repentance for the forgiveness of sins (Mk. 1:1-4).

"The voice of one crying out in the wilderness; 'Prepare the way in the wilderness; 'Prepare the way of the Lord, make his paths straight. 5 Every valley shall be filled and every mountain and hill shall be made low, and the crooked shall be made straight, and the rough ways made smooth; 6 and all flesh shall see the salvation of God.'" (Lk. 3:1-6).

I began my use of *Mark* in *Luke*, chapter three. I omitted Mark's first sentence about "beginning" because I began with the Infancy Stories (Lk. 1-2). Just as I placed them in political and religious contexts (Lk. 1:5), so I placed the start of the story of the adult Jesus in political and religious contexts (Lk. 3:1-2). What God did in Jesus was to impact the Empire. It "was not done in a corner" (Acts 26:26).

Further, Mark credits the quotations from the Hebrew scriptures to Isaiah (Mk. 1:2-3). However, verse 3 is from Malachi. I correct this by omitting verse 2 (though I use it later, Lk. 7:27). In the use of Isaiah, Mark quotes only Isaiah 40:3. I extend the quotation to include Isaiah 40:4-5 also (Lk. 3:4-6). Why? I wanted to emphasize that in Jesus "all flesh shall see the salvation of God." Jesus was good news "for all the people" - Jews and Gentiles.

To compare what I wrote with *Mark* yields much fruit in understanding my updated story of Jesus and of emphases that I wanted to make for my readers in my time. This was part of the continuing interpretive work of the Holy Spirit. Just as in the Hebrew Bible, later scripture interpreted earlier scripture, that same process went on among early Christians like Mark and me, in and for our communities to further the good news. It is a process that continued and needs to continue in the church's life and witness always.

A selection of Jesus' teachings

Followers of a great teacher often want to preserve and extend their master's teaching. Jesus' followers wanted to do the same. Those teachings, like stories of his deeds, were first transmitted orally, but as time went on the need came to write them down. This selection of Jesus' teachings was one of my sources.[15]

Mark includes some of Jesus' teachings, but apparently he did not know this selection. With my use of it, I was able to include and weave in many more of Jesus' teachings.

After writing *Luke-Acts* I learned about *The Gospel of Matthew*. The writer also used this teachings source, but both of us used it in our own way. For instance, we both tell of Jesus' three temptations (Lk. 4:1-13; Mt. 4:1-11), but my ordering of them differs from Matthew. The key importance I place on Jerusalem and the temple in *Luke-Acts* caused me to emphasize the temple temptation by ending with it.

Further, the way we included and reshaped Jesus' teaching, in Matthew's "sermon on the mount" (Mt. 5-7) and my "sermon on the plain" (Lk. 6:20-49), differs; and I wove in elsewhere in *Luke* (in chapters 11, 12, 13, 14, 16) parts of what Matthew included in chapters 5-7. To place *Matthew* in parallel columns along with *Mark* and *Luke* helps to show what they have in common and where they differ.[16] Such comparisons lead one to discern the teachings source that lies back of Matthew's and my writings.

Why did this source finally disappear?[17] Once the teachings were woven into the whole witness to Jesus, there was no longer any need for it. We cannot divorce Jesus' teachings from the entire story. They need to be woven into the whole fabric. To see Jesus only as a teacher is to miss his deeds, his death and resurrection, his final coming.[18] Our witness needs to be to all of these.

Infancy stories

Why did I include the infancy stories (Lk. 1-2)?[19] Why did I not just follow Mark and begin with Jesus' baptism? Well, I wanted to proclaim that Jesus was Messiah and Lord, not only from his baptism but from his birth as well. I wanted to include the whole of his life.

Early Christians first saw Jesus as Messiah, Lord, Son of God, in his death and resurrection (see Acts 2:31,36).[20] Without the resurrection we probably never would have heard the rest of the story. So it was through the lens of Jesus' death and resurrection that early Christians looked back on his earlier ministry. Through that lens they could see him also as Messiah, Lord, Son of God in the deeds and words of his ministry back to his baptism. In the Infancy Stories I wanted to push those titles back to his conception and birth. In words to Mary,

> "And now, you will conceive in your womb and bear a son, and you will name him Jesus. He will be great, and will be called the *Son of the Most High*. . . The Holy Spirit will come upon you, and the power of the Most High will overshadow you; therefore the child to be born will be holy, he will be called *Son of God*" (Lk. 1:32,35).

In words to the shepherds,

> "Do not be afraid; for see - I am bringing you good news of great joy
> for all the people: to you is born this day in the city of David a *Savior*,
> who is the *Messiah*, the *Lord*" (Lk. 2:10-11).

In my community we applied titles to Jesus in the Infancy Stories that early Christians first applied to Jesus after his resurrection. We proclaimed that God's Spirit was at work in him from the very beginning of his earthly life.

There was something else I wanted to do. If I tied in later titles to Jesus' birth, I also wanted to tie in earlier parts of the Hebrew heritage and show Jesus' Hebrew roots.

Zechariah, John the baptist's father, was a Jewish priest. The angel's message to him links John to the prophet Elijah. Zechariah's song taps into Hebrew history to include David and Abraham and proclaim God's salvation, forgiveness, mercy, light, and peace (Lk. 1:67-79). Jesus' birth ties into the city of David, Bethlehem, and fulfills prophetic expectation (Lk. 2:4; Mic. 2:8).

Elizabeth, John's mother, like the prophet Samuel's mother Hannah, bore him miraculously in old age; and Mary's song (Lk. 1:46-55) has roots in Hannah's song (I Sam. 2:1-10). I showed Jesus and his parents to be fully observant Jews (Lk.2:21-24, 39-42).

It was important for me and my community to tie both John and Jesus into our Hebrew heritage and to sing with Mary and Zechariah songs that celebrate, both what God has done in the past and is doing in John and Jesus.

The Infancy Stories also tie into the political context (Lk. 1:5; 2:1-2). What happened with Elizabeth and Zechariah and John, with Mary and Joseph and Jesus, with Anna and Simeon, was not some backwater event. It was indeed "good news of great joy for all the people" of the Empire.

Other Material

About a fourth of the material I include in *Luke* is unique. Some of it came from oral traditions in my own community that I reshaped. Among such materials are some of Jesus' famous parables: the good Samaritan (Lk. 10:30-37), the rich fool (12:13-21), on humility (14:7-14), the lost sons (15:11-32), the unjust steward (16:1-13), the unjust judge (18:1-8), the Pharisee and the tax collector (18:9-14). They all dealt with issues I cared about in my community.

Unique also are some stories of Jesus reaching out to hurting or outcast persons: a weeping widow (7:11-1), an outcast woman (7:36-50), Martha and Mary (10:38-42), a friend at midnight (11:5-8), a women with an infirmity (13:10-17), a man with dropsy (14:1-6), the rich man and Lazarus (16:19-31), a Samaritan leper (17:11-19), a tax collector (19:1-10). From this list, one can see how much Jesus cared about hurt people.

From what I have said about my sources, you can see that my writing *Luke-Acts* was no simple matter. It included the influence of friends and church community, the availability of written sources, oral traditions. It involved the creative shaping of it all through one's mind and heart to meet the needs of one's community and the larger world of which that community is a part.

The Holy Spirit did not "inspire" me in some mechanical way to write *Luke-Acts*. God's Spirit was at work in my community and me, in our hearts and minds and with our sources, to inspire and shape a message that really can be "good news of great joy for all the people."[21]

How then did I order and shape my materials and message? I turn to this in our next conversation.

Endnotes

[1]The reference to "eyewitnesses and servants of the word" (Lk. 1:2) points to Luke as a second generation Christian. It is interesting to note the generation phenomenon among early Christians in II Tim. 1:5. The reference to Timothy's parents in Acts 16:1, as well as Luke's dominant concern for both Jews and Gentiles, shows Luke's concern for both heritages.

[2]Luke portrays that Jesus himself taught in synagogues (Lk. 4:15,16,31-32,44) and in the temple (19:47; 20:1; 21:37-38). After the resurrection, Jesus' disciples rejoice in the temple (Lk. 24:53), spend time there (Acts 2:46; 3:1,8) and teach there (5:20-21,42). Paul preached in synagogues (13:5, 14-16; 14:1; 17:1-3,10-11,16-17; 18:4,19,26), purified himself for temple sacrifice (21:26), and prayed in the temple (22:17).

[3]Luke brings the story of Paul's transformation three times in three different contexts (Acts 9:1-22; 22:1-21; 26:1-18). Note Paul's own references in Gal. 1:11-17; Phil. 3:3-11).

[4]The Jewish council at Jamnia in the late 80's C.E. made official that anyone who believed in Jesus as the Messiah was to be put out of the synagogue. *The Gospel of John* reflects this directly (Jn. 9:22; 12:42; 16:2).

[5]Lk. 1:47-55,68-79; 2:14,29-32.

[6]Lk. 11:2-4, Luke's version of the Lord's Prayer.

[7]Lk. 4:18-20; Acts 2:17-21; 8:32; 13:47.

[8]Lk. 10:25-37; 15:1-31; 18:9-14.

[9]Lk. 7:36-50; 14:12-14; 17:11-19; 19:1-10.

[10]We call the scholarly task of seeking to define these earlier oral pieces "form criticism." This takes us back into the pre-literary period of the early church before such pieces became part of written documents.

[11]All of the gospels have anonymous writers. "Mark" is the name which tradition has assigned to this gospel. Most scholars see Mark as the oldest of our biblical gospels and presuppose Luke's use of Mark. This has to do with what we call the "synoptic problem," "source criticism," and the relationship among the synoptic ("viewed together") gospels: Matthew, Mark, and Luke. Who used whom? There are a few scholars who challenge the prevailing view that Mark is the earliest gospel.

[12]Luke omits Mk. 6:45-8:26 and inserts other materials, namely Lk. 6:20-8:3; Lk. 9:51-18:14.

[13]If Mark still held to a near expectation of Jesus' final coming (*parousia* in the Greek), it may be that he saw that final coming as *the* appearance of Jesus. Mark 16:9-20 do have resurrection appearances, but scholarly work on ancient Greek manuscripts ("text criticism") clearly reveals these verses to be a later addition. Utilizing the other gospels, the writers of this addition gave another ending to what was for them an unacceptable ending in Mk. 16:8.

[14]Scholars have put together what we know as "gospel parallels" of both the Greek text and their translations. Seeing the gospels, especially the synoptic gospels, in parallel columns provides an excellent tool for comparative work on them.

[15]Scholars call this source "Q" from the German word for source, *Quelle*. This is a hypothetical document since we have no copies of it. However, though some scholars would challenge its existence, a comparative study of Matthew and Luke points in the direction of their having used such a source. Some scholars have tried to reconstruct it and to define its own theological views.

[16]Here again the use of a "gospel parallels" is invaluable.

[17]Some scholars think that non-biblical gospels like *The Gospel of Thomas* carry on this teachings source tradition. But such gospels, with only a concern for Jesus' teaching, were never included in the New Testament. We identify them more with a religious movement known as "gnosticism" ("knowing"). The

emphases there was on revealed knowledge, hence the primary concern for teaching material.

[18]The gospels hold together at least four aspects of Christology (understanding of Christ): a power Christology (Jesus' deeds), a wisdom Christology (Jesus' teaching), a passion Christology (Jesus suffering, death, and resurrection), and an apocalyptic Christology (Jesus' future coming). The various gospels interpret these differently, but each includes them all.

[19]Matthew is the only other New Testament writing to include infancy stories. Though they have some common elements, the infancy stories of Matthew (Mt. 1-2) and Luke are distinct. Paul is the only other New Testament writer to refer to Jesus' birth directly, "born of woman" (Gal. 4:4).

[20]For examples of other use of titles see Acts 5:31,42; 9:20; 13:23,33; 17:3; 26:23).

[21]In this chapter, I limit my discussion of sources to *Luke*. Since we have no materials with which to compare *Acts*, it is more difficult to pursue. Luke probably did have sources, whether oral or written, from various locations referred to in Acts, but his own shaping of the material with his own theological emphases make *Acts*, not simple history but more an historical novel. Though Paul is a great hero for Luke, the Paul of *Acts* is distinct from the Paul of his own letters.

A Time-line of Paul and the Gospels

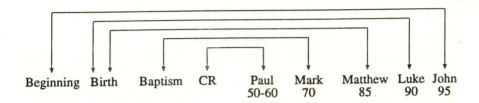

| Beginning | Birth | Baptism | CR | Paul 50-60 | Mark 70 | Matthew 85 | Luke 90 | John 95 |

In terms of Jesus' ministry, Paul's seven "undisputed" letters (Romans, 1-2 Corinthians, Galatians, Philippians, 1 Thessalonians, Philemon - others probably were written in his name after his death) focus primarily on the CR (cross and resurrection) - the love of God in the cross and the power of God for new life in the resurrection.

Mark expands the story of the cross and resurrection as the need arises at the end of the first Christian generation to include also some of Jesus' deeds and teachings and to push the story of Jesus back to his baptism.

Matthew used Mark and a teachings source ("Q"), plus other materials unique to him, to shape his gospel in his own way and push the story of Jesus back to his birth, with a genealogy that goes back to Abraham and thereby linking Jesus for his Jewish Christian readers to the whole Hebrew heritage.

Luke also uses Mark and "Q" and materials unique to him to shape his gospel in his own way, also pushing the story of Jesus back to his birth with his own infancy narratives and a genealogy back to Adam (to "humanity) for his largely Gentile Christian readers to point to Jesus as the heir of the whole human race. Matthew and Luke are the only New Testament writers to give us birth stories, though Paul does say "born of woman" (Gal. 4:4).

John (without any birth stories and with the beginning of Genesis in mind) pushes the story of Jesus back to the beginning, "In the beginning was the word" (Jn. 1:1). The *logos* (word, communication, purpose) that became a human being in Jesus was no after-thought on God's part. God's word-purpose, made flesh in Jesus (Jn. 1:14), was in the heart of God from the beginning.

The first century dates below the names are to be understood as good possibilities. Scholars still are debating some of them.

CHAPTER 3
How I Constructed My Materials

"In the first book . . . I wrote about all that Jesus did and taught from the beginning until the day when he was taken up to heaven, after giving instructions through the Holy Spirit to the apostles whom he had chosen" (Acts 1:1).

Two parts

I wrote a two-part work. The quotation from *Acts* above points immediately to this fact. For me it was not enough to write a story of Jesus' life and ministry (*Luke*). That was the message. But I needed also to write a story of how his first followers began to spread that message across the world (*Acts*).

Telling both could serve to inform and inspire people in my time to continue to share the good news. As the Holy Spirit had been at work in both Jesus and the early church, I wanted my readers to see how the Holy Spirit could be at work in them.

I did not give my two-part work the titles they now bear, *The Gospel according to Luke* and *The Acts of the Apostles*. Others attached such titles later.[1] If I were to name them, I probably would call them *The Work of the Holy Spirit in Jesus* and *The Work of the Holy Spirit in the Early Church*. I never would have called the second part *The Acts of the Apostles*. Why?

Though I do tell of some acts of the apostles Peter and John, the main actor is Paul; and for me, Paul was not an "apostle." By my definition, only the twelve were apostles. To be an apostle, one had to be a witness to both Jesus' ministry and his resurrection (see Acts 1:21-26). Paul did not fulfill the first of these criteria.[2] He was not a witness to Jesus' ministry.

But that did not prevent him, in my view, from being the most important instrument of the Holy Spirit among early Christians. Yet, he did not work as a lone individual. Others preceded him in the Christian mission, and others were with him almost constantly to share in and support his work. Christians need one another to fulfill their task of spreading good news.

So, the good news began with Jesus in the first half of my two-part work, and it advanced in the work of apostles, Paul, and others in the second. But in both it is God's Holy Spirit who was acting to empower them and who continues to empower us.

Yet I did not *begin* either *Luke* or *Acts* with these empowered missions.

Two beginnings

I began *Luke* with a statement of my purpose (Lk. 1:1-4)[3] and followed it with the Infancy Stories. I wanted to proclaim God's Spirit at work in Jesus' (as well as John the Baptist's) conception, birth, and childhood (Lk. 1:5-2:52). This preceded the Spirit's work in Jesus' mission. These stories also rooted Jesus in the Hebrew heritage and proclaimed him as Messiah, Lord, Son of God, from the beginning of his earthly life.

I began *Acts* with a need to reassert again (Acts 1:2) Jesus' commission of his disciples (Lk. 24:44-49). Such repetition reinforces how central that commission is.

Here let me explain a difference between *Luke's* end and *Acts'* beginning. In *Luke* I tell of Jesus being carried up into heaven on the day of his resurrection

(Lk. 24:51; also Acts 1:2). But in *Acts* I tell of this occurring after forty days of appearances as the risen Jesus (Acts 1:3,9).[4]

The *Luke* text ties the resurrected and ascended/exalted Jesus closely together. Precisely the risen Jesus is the exalted Lord whom the disciples worship (Lk. 24:52). The *Acts* text, however, tells of this forty-day period of Jesus' continuing instruction about God's reign. This forty-day instruction before the beginning of their ministry parallels the forty-day preparatory temptation of Jesus before his ministry.

The beginning of *Acts* also tells of the apostles' waiting for the promised power (Lk. 24:49; Acts 1:4-8). They with Jesus' brothers, mother, and some other women devoted themselves to prayer (Acts 1:12-14). They also act to replace the dead Judas, the apostle who betrayed Jesus, in order that their full number, twelve, might parallel Israel's twelve tribes and express the continuity between God's covenant communities of Israel and the church.

God's empowering Spirit in both *Luke* and *Acts* does not go to work in a vacuum. The beginnings of *Luke* and *Acts* provide the needed contexts.

Two missions

In *Luke*, Jesus' mission begins with his empowerment by the Holy Spirit.
"and the Holy Spirit descended upon him in bodily form like a dove.
And a voice came from heaven, 'You are my Son, the Beloved; with you
I am well pleased'" (Lk. 2:22).

Here I want to suggest what I think is a better translation of the last phrase: "in you I-have-willed-the-good" (the hyphenated words are one word in the original Greek).[5] This translation expresses that the Spirit empowers Jesus as an instrument of God's good will in the world. The baptism of those "baptized in the name of Jesus"[6] then also marks them as God's children and instruments of God's good will.

With my genealogy of Jesus (Lk. 3:23-38), I tie Jesus' baptism as Son of God to all of humanity (to ''Adam''). Jesus is the heir of the whole human race. God's good will in him is for all.

Yet the very one empowered by the Spirit for *good* will has to face the tempting power of *bad* will (Lk. 4:1-13). Jesus refused to misuse his identity as God's son.[7] He did not succumb to the false identities of material goods, worldly power, and fool-hardy religion. God's good will in him triumphed over bad will.

Having stood this test, ''full of the Holy Spirit,'' Jesus entered into his ministry (Lk. 4:14-15) and declared the program of his Spirit-empowered mission by reading from Isaiah in his hometown synagogue.

> ''The Spirit of the Lord is upon me, because he has anointed me to bring
>   good news to the poor.
> He has sent me to proclaim release to the captives and recovery of sight to the
>   blind,
> to let the oppressed go free,
> and to proclaim the year of the Lord's favor'' (4:18-19).

This set the liberating tone of his mission: to free people from all the many forms of human bondage that thwart their living out the fullness of their lives as children of God's good will. That mission in turn becomes the mission of Jesus' followers. This is what I wanted my readers to understand and take up.

In *Acts* I tell of the mission of Jesus' first followers, empowered by the Spirit at Pentecost.[8] John the Baptist promised that he (Jesus) ''will baptize you with the Holy Spirit and fire'' (Lk. 3:16). Jesus promised that ''you will receive power when the Holy Spirit has come upon you; and you will be my witnesses in Jerusalem, in all Judea and Samaria, and to the ends of the earth'' (Acts 1:8). In the Pentecost story, that promise is fulfilled (Acts 2:2-4).[9]

I make the point that Jews came to Jerusalem to celebrate Pentecost ''from every nation under heaven'' (see Acts 2:9-10), together with proselytes (converts to Judaism), Cretans, and Arabs. Pentecost provided an international audience for telling the good news. People from the ''ends of the earth'' came to Jerusalem and could take the message home with them.

But it is important to note that such an international mission did not begin with the early Christians. It was the mission of Israel as well. To tell of their mission, early Christians quote a text where God speaks through the prophet Isaiah:

> "I have set you to be a light to the Gentiles (nations), so that you may
> bring salvation to the ends of the earth" (Acts 13:47, quoting Is. 49:6).

Further, the Spirit-empowered speaking in tongues (*glossolalia*, Acts 2:4) was not ecstatic speech beyond human language. It was the power to speak in known languages, so people from everywhere could respond, "we hear, each of us, in our own native language" (Acts 2:8). God knows no language barriers in the mission "to the ends of the earth."

Two journeys

I order my materials to include two major journeys: Jesus' journey from Galilee to Jerusalem (in *Luke*) and the journey of the Christian mission from Jerusalem to Rome (in *Acts*). Jesus and his followers were people on the move with a message. Several times I refer to Christians as belonging to "the Way."[10]

In the expectation of some Hebrew prophets, Jerusalem was to be the center of a new world order of abundance, security, gladness (see Is. 65:17-25; Zech. 8:1-23). Peace was to flow from Jerusalem to the nations (Is. 2:2-4; Mic. 4:1-3; Zech. 9:9-10). For me, Jerusalem meant the climax of Jesus' journey and the beginning of a new journey to bring a message of joy and peace for the world.

During Jesus' ministry, his disciples also had a journey. In *Luke*, when Jesus sent out his twelve disciples to proclaim God's reign and to heal, he said, "Take nothing for your *journey*" (Lk. 9:3). To show the need for more people in an expanding mission, I also tell of Jesus' command to the seventy to "Go" (Lk. 10:3).[11]

After his ministry in Galilee (Lk. 4:14-9:50), I emphasize that "when the days drew near for him to be taken up, he set his face to go to Jerusalem" (Lk.

9:51). I made the material that follows a part of Jesus' journey to Jerusalem (Lk. 9:51-19:28). I reemphasize the journey to Jerusalem five times along the way[12] and bring Jesus' words that "it is impossible for a prophet to be killed outside of Jerusalem" (Lk. 13:33).

Jerusalem, the geographical center of the Hebrew heritage, had to be the end of the journey and the place of his final ministry, suffering, death, resurrection, and exaltation. It had to be the place to end one journey and begin another.

Near the beginning of *Acts* the risen Jesus says, "and you will be my witnesses in Jerusalem, in all Judea and Samaria, and to the ends of the earth" (Acts 1:8). At Jerusalem begins a journey that will take witnesses across the Empire and conclude with Paul's final journey to Rome. There Paul preaches and teaches "with all boldness and without hindrance" (Acts 28:31). For me that meant to impact the center of political power with God's good news.

As the story of the geographically expanding journey proceeded, I stopped five times to summarize its progress.

> "The word of God continued to spread; the number of the disciples increased greatly in Jerusalem, and a great many of the priests became obedient to the faith" (Acts 6:7).

> "Meanwhile the church through Judea, Galilee, and Samaria had peace and was built up. Living in the fear of the Lord and in the comfort of the Holy Spirit, it increased in numbers" (Acts 9:31).

> "But the word of God continued to advance and gain adherents" (Acts 12:24).

> "So the churches were strengthened in the faith and increased in numbers daily" (Acts 16:5).

> "So the word of the Lord grew mightily and prevailed" (Acts 19:20).

Jesus and the early Christians were people of "The Way." They journeyed to spread the "word" from Galilee to Jerusalem and from Jerusalem to Rome. These journeys helped to order my story.

Two turning points

I present two major turning points. In *Luke* it is when Jesus "set his face to go to Jerusalem" (Lk. 9:51, beginning his journey). In *Acts* it is when the mission begins to open up to the Gentiles (Acts 10).

Before the turning point in *Luke*, I tell the story of Jesus' ministry of preaching, teaching, healing, and feeding in the region of Galilee. After it comes the story of Jesus' ministry on his way to Jerusalem with his final end always there in the background. Before the turning point, Jesus sent out his *twelve* disciples to share his ministry (Lk. 9:1-6). After it he sent out *seventy* for an expanded ministry (Lk. 10:1-20).

Before the turning point in *Acts*, the disciples (all Jews) shared in a preaching, teaching, healing, worshiping, caring ministry among Jews in Jerusalem. There was opposition, yet "the number of disciples increased greatly in Jerusalem" (Acts 6:7).

Persecution of the Jerusalem church forced some disciples out into Judea to preach there; and Philip had a ministry to a traveling Jewish Ethiopian. Saul (Paul),[13] a persecutor of Christians, had his Damascus Road "turn around" and became persecuted himself. Yet "the church through Judea, Galilee, and Samaria had peace and was built up" (Acts 9:31). Peter's successful ministry in Lydda and Joppa followed (Acts 9:36-43).

Up to this point, the mission, though expanding, was confined to Jews and their Samaritan cousins. (The Samaritans, rejected by Jews as heretics and foreigners, were the offspring of Jews who had intermarried with non-Jews after the Babylonian exile and established their own center of worship and religious beliefs.) After this point comes the breakthrough to Gentiles. As I tell the story, Paul's *call* by God "to bring my name before Gentiles" (Acts 9:15) already has occurred, but it is Peter's breakthrough experience with the Roman soldier

Cornelius that initiates the Gentile mission (Acts 10-11). "God has given even to the Gentiles the repentance that leads to life" (Acts 11:18).

The turning point for Jesus moves him toward Jerusalem through suffering and death to God's triumph in the resurrection. The turning point for his followers move them from a more limited mission to one that meant good news of great joy for all people.

Two trials

The words about the turning point for Jesus already anticipate his end, "When the days drew near for him *to be taken up*, he set his face to Jerusalem" (Lk. 9:51). The story of his final days in Jerusalem begins with the end of that journey (Lk. 19:28) and includes his trial before Pilate, the Roman governor. I understood it as a trial instigated by some religious leaders whom Jesus had challenged and provoked.

> "When the scribes and chief priests realized that he had told this parable against them, they wanted to lay hands on him at that very hour, but they feared the people. So they watched him and sent spies who pretended to be honest, in order to trap him by what he said, so as to hand him over to the jurisdiction and authority of the governor" (Lk.20:19-20).

The story finally does lead to that "handing over."

> "Then the assembly rose as one body and brought Jesus before Pilate. They began to accuse him, saying, 'We found this man perverting our nation, forbidding us to pay taxes to the emperor, and saying that he himself is the Messiah, a king" (Lk. 23:1-2).

Yet, I emphasize that Pilate declared Jesus innocent *three times* (Lk. 23:4,14,22). The Roman soldier at Jesus' crucifixion also declared him innocent; and Pilate's political underling, King Herod, refuses to accept the accusations (Lk. 23:10-11).

My telling of the story is longer than Mark's because I wanted to emphasize Jesus' innocence of any charges of political insurrection against Rome. Pilate finally gives in (Lk. 23:23-25), but Jesus' innocence remains.

Jesus was faithful to his mission. He was and is God's Son, the Messiah, the Lord, the Savior (Lk. 2:11), the one in whom God's good news of great joy was present for all people.

Toward the end of *Acts*, Paul also stands on trial. He has nearly finished his mission in the northeasterly Mediterranean world (Acts 13-19) and begins his journey, led by the Spirit, first to Jerusalem and then on to Rome (Acts 19:21). On his journey, I tell of his words to the Ephesian elders.

> "And now, as a captive to the Spirit, I am on my way to Jerusalem, not knowing what will happen to me there, except that the Holy Spirit testifies to me in every city that imprisonment and persecutions are waiting for me. But I do not count my life of any value to myself, if only I may finish my course and the ministry that I received from the Lord Jesus, to testify to the good news of God's grace" (Acts 20:22-24).

Like Jesus, Paul had to face plots by religious leaders against him (Acts 20:3; 21:11,27-31). Yet a Roman tribune saved him from possible death (Acts 21:31-36; 23:10), and his Roman citizenship helped him (Acts 22:25-29).

Defending himself, Paul appeared before two Roman governors (Acts 24-25), but he finally appealed to go before the emperor in Rome. Yet one of the governors said that Paul "had done nothing to deserve death" (Acts 25:25); and others who heard his defense said, "This man is doing nothing to deserve death or imprisonment." "This man could have been set free if he had not appealed to the emperor" (Acts 26:31-32).

Both Jesus and Paul stood on trial, both innocent of any political charges against them. They only were faithful proclaimers of God's reign. That reign breaks through any existing religious establishment that excludes people from God's one human family. Their challenge of religious authorities, who wanted to retain power for themselves, caused such leaders to oppose them.

Jesus' trial does lead to his death, but God raised him up and made him both Lord and Messiah (Acts 2:36). On trial before a governor, Paul said, "It is about the resurrection of the dead that I am on trial before you today" (Acts 24:21); and in another defense Paul asked, "Why is it thought incredible by any of you that God raises the dead?" (Acts 26:8).

> "To this day I have had help from God, and so I stand here, testifying to both small and great, saying nothing but what the prophets and Moses said would take place: that the Messiah must suffer, and that, by being the first to rise from the dead, he would proclaim light both to our people and the Gentiles" (Acts 26:22-23).

When I put *Luke-Acts* together, I wanted to proclaim God's power for new life in raising Jesus from the dead. It is a power that is victorious through all trials. It is a power finally that triumphs over all religious and political opposition.

Given the fact that the religious opponents of Jesus and Paul had and interpreted the same Hebrew scriptures as they did, how did early Christians and I interpret those scriptures? This is the focus of our next conversation.

Endnotes

[1]This happened in the second century, and these second century traditions became the standard titles.

[2]Paul does call himself an apostle. He bases it upon the risen Lord's appearance to and commission of him (I Cor. 15:8-9; Gal. 1:11-12). Luke does slip and call him an apostle with others in one text, Acts 14:4).

[3]This beginning parallels other literary beginnings at the time of *Luke-Acts* and suggests Luke's familiarity with them.

[4]The number forty has a long tradition behind it: the rain for forty days and nights in the flood story (Gen. 7:12); Moses' forty days on the mountain (Ex. 34:28); Israel's wilderness wanderings for forty years (Dt. 8:2-6); Elijah's forty days of flight to the mountain (I Kings 19:4-8). The number has a symbolic sense of fullness.

[5]The Greek *eudokesa* is an aorist (simple past), active verb. It belongs to the same family as the word translated "good will" in Lk. 2:14 (KJV), "gracious will" in Lk. 10:21 (NRSV), "good pleasure" in Lk. 12:32 (NRSV).

[6]In Acts people are baptized "in the name of Jesus" (Acts 2:38; 8:16; 10:48; 19:5). Early Christians used various formulae.

[7]Note the devil's words, "*If* you are the Son of God" (Lk. 4:3,9).

[8]Luke is the only New Testament writer to tell us the Pentecost story. Pentecost is a Jewish harvest festival, also called the Feast of Weeks. It falls 50 (*pente*) days after Passover and 50 days after Easter.

[9]The words "breath," "wind," "spirit," all are translations of the one Greek word *pneuma*.

[10]See Acts 9:2; 19:9,23; 22:4; 24:14,22; note also Acts 16:17; 18:25-26; Lk. 1:76,79; 10:3. The Greek word *hodos*, "way," also can be translated

"journey," Lk. 2:44; 9:3; Acts 1:12; or "road," Lk. 14:23; 24:32; or "path," Lk. 8:5,12.

[11]The number 70 recalls Moses' choice of seventy elders (Num. 11:16-25).

[12]Lk. 13:22,33; 17:11; 18:31; 19:28.

[13]As a Jewish person who grew up in a Greek context, he had two names. Saul was his Hebrew name, Paul his Greek name. Saul did not become Paul when he believed in Jesus.

CHAPTER 4

My Interpretation
of the Scriptures

"Then beginning with Moses and all the prophets, he interpreted to them
the things about himself in all the scriptures" (Lk. 24:27).

The Community of Israel

The "Bible" of my community was a Greek translation of the Hebrew
scriptures - what you know as the Old Testament. These writings arose in Israel's
life over nearly a thousand years of Hebrew history. Though oral traditions
preceded them, once written down the Israelites could use them in their worship
and life to nourish, guide, and challenge them in their continuing history. These
writings were the scriptures for us early Christians too.

God's Spirit was at work in the life and community of Israel long before
there were any writings. The writings emerged in response to God and to the
needs of the community. They didn't drop out of heaven. The word translated
"testament" or "covenant" referred first to the covenant or testament *community*
before it referred to covenant or testament *writings*. From the covenant community
of Israel came the Hebrew covenant writings.

Sometimes I refer to them as ''the scriptures,'' sometimes as ''the law and the prophets'' (Lk. 16:16), sometimes as ''the law of Moses, the prophets, and the psalms'' (Lk. 24:44). The last one shows that the Hebrew scriptures were divided into three parts: the law (the first five writings, Gen.-Deut.), the prophets, and the writings. The process of their becoming Israel's official scripture (the canon, ''measuring stick'') covered hundreds of years,[1] though they were part of Israel's life through many years before they became official, canonical writings.

Why did these writings become Israel's canon? I think that the main reason was their capacity to sustain and nourish, guide and correct, challenge and inspire Israel through the years. They became authoritative because people experienced God's Spirit at work in their midst as they listened to and learned from them.

Israel did not exist to witness to or point to itself. Israel existed to witness to God and God's purposes. Nor did Israel's scriptures exist to witness to or point to themselves. They exist to point to the living God and God's purposes. So their scriptures helped Israel again and again to keep their priorities straight and be faithful to God's call as a light to the nations.

On the basis of the Hebrew scriptures, Jesus challenged his own synagogue community to a larger vision of God - a God who cared for other peoples beyond themselves (Lk. 4:16-30). His challenge got him into trouble, but he would not let his own people ''make God too small.'' I wanted to follow Jesus in that vision and to interpret the Hebrew scriptures as he did.

The community of the church

The Hebrew Bible was the scripture for all of the earliest Christians. It was part of their life and worship, and they interpreted Jesus in the light of it.

But in my time, there were those who wanted to separate Israel, its history, and its scriptures from the church. They wanted to separate the creating God from the redeeming God. They saw creation as the evil product of a bad God with human beings trapped in a bad creation. In their view, the good God then comes to free people from this entrapping darkness and lift them to the realm of light.

This happens by their grasping a system of knowledge that emanates from this good God.

The Greek word for "knowledge" is *gnosis*, and the religion I have described is called gnosticism. Gnostics wanted to reshape and incorporate Jesus' teachings into that system of knowledge, but they wanted to keep him from truly entering into the evil (as they saw it) of the created world. They could not see him coming *in carne*, in the flesh of this world.

But the very heart of the good news was that Jesus was born into this world. Gnosticism undercut the very foundation of Christian faith. I wanted none of that. Jesus was Jewish and born in this world (God's good creation). He was inseparably related to the God of creation and the community of Israel, its history and its scriptures. That means that his followers have that same connection.

This is why my writings are so full of that connection. I refer to the Hebrew scriptures at least 60 times each in *Luke* and *Acts*. I saw it as a major part of my task to relate both Jesus and the early church to those scriptures. The scriptures were indispensable in helping to interpret Jesus and his mission, as well as the church and its mission. Early Christians cited Israel's mission to express their own.

> "I have set you to be a light for the Gentiles, so that you may bring salvation to the ends of the earth" (Is. 49:6, quoted in Acts 13:47).

The communities of Israel and the church belong together.

The infancy stories

The infancy stories (Lk. 1-2) have strong links to the Hebrew scriptures. The songs of Mary and Zechariah have roots there. Mary's expectant song shows connections to Hannah's song at Samuel's birth (1 Sam. 2:1-10). Here are two examples.

Mary: "My soul magnifies the Lord" (Lk. 1:47).
Hannah: "My heart exults in the Lord" (1 Sam. 2:1).

Mary: "He has brought down the mighty from their thrones,
                      and lifted up the lowly" (Lk. 1:52).
Hannah: "he brings low, he also exalts. He raises up the poor from the
                      dust; he lifts the needy from the ask heap, to make them
                      sit with princes and inherit a seat of honor (1 Sam. 2:8).

Mary sings of God's mercy to Israel and God's promise to Abraham and his descendants forever (Lk. 1:54-55; see Gen. 17:7).

Zechariah's song looks back on God's favor and mercy toward Israel with references to David, the prophets, and Abraham (Lk. 1:67-75) and lifts up such important scriptural words as salvation, forgiveness, mercy, light, peace (Lk. 1:76-79). Simeon's song also picks up the scriptural words of peace, salvation, and light (Lk. 2:29-32).

The infancy stories link John the Baptist and Jesus to Israel's scriptures, not only in their adult ministries but even in the prenatal and natal periods of their lives. God's deeds in the past, as witnessed to in the Hebrew scriptures, inform and inspire an understanding of what God is doing in the present to scatter the proud, lift up the lowly, fill the hungry, and guide feet into the way of peace (see Lk. 1:51-53,79).

The temptation of Jesus

Jesus challenges the devil's temptation by quoting from the Hebrew scriptures. He appeals to his heritage to fight against the power of evil that wanted to undercut his identity and mission as God's Son.

In the temptation to turn stones to bread, he responds,

"It is written, 'One does not live by bread alone'" (Lk. 4:4 from Deut. 8:3).

In the temptation to receive glory and authority over the world's kingdoms in exchange for worshiping the devil, he says,

"Worship the Lord your God, and serve only him" (Lk. 4:8 from Deut. 6:13).

In the temptation to trust God to protect him in throwing himself down from the temple's pinnacle, the devil first quotes scripture:

"for it is written, 'He will command his angels concerning you, to protect you' and 'On their hands they will bear you up, so that you will not dash your foot against a stone'" (Lk. 4:10-11 from Ps. 91:11-12).

But Jesus replies,

"It is said, 'Do not put the Lord your God to the test'" (Lk. 4:12 from Deut. 6:16).

The devil uses scriptural authority too, but it is a misuse. One cannot test God to save one from foolhardy action. That is a false dependence on God's protecting care.

So I tell of Jesus' own use of his rich scriptural heritage from the past to meet present evil with resisting power. To use scripture is to tap into the experience of people in the past in order to be faithful to God's mission in the present.

The mission of Jesus

Jesus' mission is rooted in the Hebrew scriptures, but so also is the mission of John the Baptist, who prepared his way. Though the prophet Isaiah had his own historical situation in view some 500 years B.C.E., we applied the text also to John.

"The voice of one crying out in the wilderness: 'Prepare the way of the Lord, make his paths straight.
Every valley shall be filled, and every mountain and hill shall be made low, and the crooked shall be made straight, and the rough places smooth; and all flesh shall see the salvation of God'" (Lk. 3:4-6 from Is. 40:3-5).

John's preparation led on to Jesus' baptism and his empowerment by the Spirit for his mission.

At his baptism the words from heaven, "You are my Son, the Beloved" (Lk. 3:22) echo a psalm's earlier words about Israel's king, "You are my son" (Ps. 2:7; note also "son" references in Ex. 4:22 and Hos. 11:1).

With Jesus empowered by the Spirit at his baptism, I tell of Jesus' first words about his mission. He speaks of it in the words of the prophet Isaiah. Israel's mission in the past becomes his mission in the present.

> "The Spirit of the Lord is upon me, because he has anointed me to bring
> good news to the poor.
> He has sent me to proclaim release to the captives and recovery of sight to the
> blind, to let the oppressed go free, to proclaim the year of the Lord's
> favor" (Luke 4:18-19, quoting selectively from Is. 61:1-2; 58:6).

Jesus then says, "Today this scripture has been fulfilled in your hearing" (Lk. 4:21). He brings Israel's mission in the past to its fullness in his mission in the present.

Yet that is not the end of the story in Luke 4. As Jesus read and interpreted the scripture in his hometown synagogue, at first "all spoke well of him" (Lk. 4:22). But when he pointed to their scripture's witness to God's feeding and healing of people in the territories of Israel's earlier enemies (Lk. 4:26-27 from 1 Kings 17:8-16; 2 Kings 5:1-14), they "drove him out of town . . . so they might hurl him off the cliff" (Lk. 4:29).

They wanted to confine God's good news to themselves. Jesus would not let them. God did not limit "good news to the poor" to them. It was for "all flesh," for all people. Jesus challenged narrow and exclusive views. It got him into trouble and finally killed him. He died the way he did, because he lived the way he did.

But his mission was not new. God's mission in him was rooted in God's mission in Israel; and it is words from Israel's scriptural heritage that Jesus used to articulate his own mission. "He interpreted to them the things about himself in all the scriptures" (Lk. 24:27).

The problem of the cross

A *crucified* Messiah? The cross was a *skandalon*, a scandal, an offense, a stumbling block.[2] A crucified Messiah was a contradiction. The expected Messiah was to be a figure of power and glory, not one who died a criminal's death on a cross.

We early Christians could understand Jesus as Messiah and Lord in terms of resurrection (Acts 2:32-36). Jews (at least the Pharisees) saw resurrection of the dead as belonging to the new age of the Messiah. But that age was to be one of victorious power and life, not humiliating defeat and death. A *crucified* Messiah? Never!

What were we to do with the cross? We turned to our Hebrew scriptures to see if they could help. I tell also how Jesus relied on the scriptures to interpret his suffering. The risen Jesus speaks to the two disciples on the Emmaus road.

> "And he said to them, 'Oh, how foolish you are, and slow of heart to believe all that the prophets have declared! Was it not necessary that the Messiah should suffer these things and then enter into his glory?' The beginning with Moses and all the prophets, he interpreted to them the things about himself in all the scriptures" (Lk. 24:25-27).

The risen Jesus also speaks to his disciples in Jerusalem.

> "Then he opened their minds to understanding the scriptures, and he said to them, 'Thus it is written, that the Messiah is to suffer and to rise from the dead on the third day'" (Lk. 24:45-46).

I sound the connection between Jesus' death and the scriptures several times.

> "Then he took the twelve aside and said to them, 'See, we are going up to Jerusalem, and everything that is written about the Son of man by the prophets will be accomplished'" (Lk. 18:31).

> "For I tell you that this scripture must be fulfilled in me, 'And he was among the lawless'; and indeed what is written about me is being fulfilled" (Lk. 22:37, referring to Is. 53:12).

In *Acts*, Peter says,

"In this way God fulfilled what he had foretold through all the prophets,
that his Messiah would suffer" (Acts 3:18).

Philip helps an Ethiopian eunuch to relate his reading of Isaiah to Jesus.

"Like a sheep he was led to the slaughter, and like a lamb silent before
   its shearer, so he does not open his mouth.
In his humiliation justice was denied him. Who can describe his generation? For
   his life is taken away from the earth" (Acts 8:32-33, quoting Is. 53:7-8).

Paul, in the synagogue in Thessalonica,

"argued with them from the scriptures, explaining and proving that it was
necessary for the Messiah to suffer and to rise from the dead, and saying,
'This is the Messiah, Jesus whom I am proclaiming to you'" (Acts 17:2-
3).

Apollos, in Achaia

"powerfully refuted the Jews in public, showing by the scriptures that the
Messiah is Jesus" (Acts 18:28).

Such texts show how we early Christians found support in the Hebrew Bible for
a Messiah who would suffer and die.

How could we rightly connect texts from earlier periods to the time of
Jesus? Isaiah, for instance, had its own historical setting some 500 years earlier.
Then *Israel*, or a part of Israel, was the suffering one.

We believed that the same living God was at work in both Israel and Jesus.
God worked in the midst of suffering and death in both. When we read the
scriptures, they gave us a lens to see that the way God worked in suffering in the
past could illuminate our understanding of Jesus' suffering. We even could see
Jesus' suffering as fulfilling those texts (Acts 3:18) and as part of God's plan to
raise him up (Acts 2:23-24; note Is. 52:13).

Falsely accused, Jesus died the death of a criminal. True to his mission of
caring for people and of challenging those who didn't, he had to face hostility and
death. Yet in his suffering and death, he entered into and identified with all human

suffering; and in God's raising him from the dead, new life, not suffering and death, had the last word.

We came to see that God works in the suffering and death that others inflict on God's servants. God's raising Jesus helped us to see that out of our struggle and suffering and death can come new creation and new life. The Hebrew scriptures helped us finally to see the cross, not as a problem but a power, God's power for life in the midst of death. Jesus was and is God's Messiah, crucified and risen from the dead.

The speeches in Acts

I present many speeches in *Acts* as part of the Christian mission. Several strongly link Jesus and the church's mission to the Hebrew scriptures.

Peter's sermon at Pentecost ties the prophet Joel's words to the outpouring of the Spirit and the prophetic mission of both sons and daughters, women and men (Acts 2:17-21; Joel 2:28-30). He gives scriptural support to God's raising Jesus (Acts 2:22- 32; Ps. 16:8-11) and to God's making Jesus Lord (Acts 2:33-36; Ps. 110:1).

Stephen's long speech (Acts 7:2-53) recounts stories of Abraham, Isaac, Jacob, Joseph, Moses, Aaron, Joshua, David, and Solomon. He quotes from Amos 5:25-27 to challenge false worship (Acts 7:39-43) and Isaiah 66:1-2 to challenge confining God to "houses made with human hands" (Acts 7:47-50). Like Jesus, his challenge cost him his life (Acts 7:54-60).

Paul quotes Psalm 2:7 ("You are my Son, today I have begotten you") to support Jesus as fulfilling God's promise (Acts 13:33). He quotes Psalm 16:10 ("You will not let your Holy One experience corruption") to support God's raising Jesus (Acts 13:35); and sounds a warning with a quotation from Habakkuk 1:5 (Acts 13:41).

Many of Paul's own Jewish people did believe (Acts 13:42), but others "were filled with jealousy; and blaspheming, they contradicted what was spoken by Paul" (Acts 13:45).

For Paul, this rejection led to a "turning to the Gentiles," and he supports that turn with a scriptural quotation. Hebrew scripture itself supports the Gentile mission.   "I have set you to be a light for the Gentiles, so that you
may bring salvation to the ends of the earth" (Acts 13:47
from Is. 49:6; note also Acts 15:16-17).

These speeches in *Acts* show how we early Christians rooted our proclamation of Jesus in the Hebrew scriptures. The God at work in Israel is the same God at work in Jesus for good news.

The love commandment

The story of a lawyer, to whom Jesus tells the parable of the good Samaritan (Lk. 10:25-37), contains an important link to the Hebrew scriptures. It begins this way.

"Just then a lawyer stood up to test Jesus. 'Teacher,' he said, 'what must I do to inherit eternal life?' He said to him, 'What is written in the law? What do you read there?' He answered, 'You shall love the Lord your God with all your heart, and with all your soul, and with all your strength, and with all your mind; and your neighbor as yourself.' And he said to him, 'You have given the right answer; do this, and you will live'' (Lk. 10:25-28).

The love commandment comes from two different scriptural texts: Deuteronomy 6:5 (loving God) and Leviticus 19:18 (loving the neighbor).[3] This *triple* love commandment (God, neighbor, self) summarizes the heart of relationships with God, with others, and with ourselves.

In my story of the love commandment, the lawyer (a lawyer who dealt with religious law) asks Jesus, "And who is my neighbor?" (vs. 29). Then Jesus told the parable. Parables intend to confront the hearer with her/his own life and call for decision on how to act.

After he tells the parable, Jesus actually changes the lawyer's question from "who is my neighbor?" to "to whom am I neighbor?" He asks the lawyer,

"Which of these three (priest, Levite, Samaritan) do you think was a

neighbor to the man who fell into the hands of robbers?'' He said, "The
one who showed him mercy.'' Jesus said to him, "Go and do likewise''
(Lk. 10:36-37).

The question, "who is my neighbor,'' calls for explaining a word. The question,
"to whom am I neighbor,'' calls for acting on need.

The quotations from Deuteronomy and Leviticus are not discussions about
love. They are calls to act with love. But on what are such calls based?

Earlier words in Deuteronomy provide the base: "I am the Lord your God,
who brought you out of the land of Egypt, out of the house of bondage'' (Deut.
5:6). God's liberating deed becomes the basis for our loving. Our love is *response*
to what God has done. We love God because God first loved us.

Earlier words in Leviticus provide another base: "You shall be holy; for
I the Lord your God am holy'' (Lev. 19:2). Holy can mean "set apart,'' but what
sets God apart is God's integrity, God's wholeness. God's holiness involves God's
whole-making, hurt-healing, life-renewing, right-doing. God is a loving neighbor
to us. Our being a loving neighbor is *response* to God, who calls us to meet
human hurts with mercy.

This chapter has shown how indispensable the Hebrew scriptures are to
understanding Jesus and the early Christian mission. Jesus himself interpreted the
scriptures and it made hearts burn (Lk. 24:32). Past history came alive to nurture
present history with good news.

To speak of history, how did I understand the sweep of history into which
Jesus came? I shall discuss this in our next conversation.

Endnotes

[1]The law or *Torah* became canon about 400 B.C.E., the prophets about 250 B.C.E., and the writings about 100 C.E. Their use in the community of course preceded their official acceptance by many, many years. Due to the fact that so many Jews spoke Greek, the Hebrew Scriptures were translated into Greek about 250 B.C.E. in what we know as the Septuagint.

[y]Luke uses the term *skandalon* in Lk. 17:1. He does not use it with reference to the cross. The most powerful treatment of the cross as *skandalon* comes in I Cor. 1:22-25.

[3]Parallel texts on the love commandment occur in Mk. 12:28-34 and Mt. 22:34-40. However, in both the lawyer's question is about the greatest commandment, not about eternal life.

CHAPTER 5

My Understanding of History

"after investigating everything from the very first. . ." (Lk. 1:3)

Jesus as history's lens

In my understanding of time and history, I start with what God has done in Jesus. When I begin *Luke* by referring to "the events that have been fulfilled among us" (Lk. 1:1), I mean Jesus' life and ministry, death and resurrection. For me, Jesus fulfills the past, gives purpose to the present, and anticipates the future. He provides a lens for looking both backward and forward and for seeing life today.

I move *backward* to "Adam" in his genealogy (Lk.23-38). I tell how Jesus himself looks *back* and "interpreted to them the things about himself in all the scriptures" (Lk. 24:27,45). He looks *back* to Isaiah to interpret his own mission (Lk. 4:16-21). From Jesus' standpoint, I look back on what God has done in the time that preceded him. This lets me view the past in light of him, and lets past witnesses interact with and help interpret our witness in the present.

He also is the lens to look toward the future. The crucial part of that lens here is Jesus' resurrection. Resurrection of the dead was not a new idea in Jesus'

time. The Jewish party of the Pharisees already believed in the future resurrection
of the dead (see Lk. 14:14; 20:34-38; Acts 23:6-8; 24:21).

But with *Jesus'* resurrection, that future hope became present. For us,
God's power to raise Jesus from the dead transformed a future hope into a present
reality. I viewed all time and history after Jesus' resurrection in this light.

God's power to give new life to Jesus gave us the basis to see God's life-
giving power at work in all the history that followed it. God not only raised Jesus
from the dead in the past. He is alive forevermore! And it is the risen Jesus,
Messiah and Lord, who commissions his disciples for their mission in that
unfolding history (Lk. 24:46-47; Acts 1:8).

But what about the future? As the Messiah, Jesus already has come (Acts
2:36). Yet in one text, Jesus as Messiah has still to come.[1] Peter preached,

> "Repent therefore, and turn to God so that your sins may be wiped out,
> so that times of refreshing may come from the presence of the Lord, that
> he may send the Messiah appointed for you, that is, Jesus, who must
> remain in heaven until the time of universal restoration (restoration of all
> things) that God announced long ago through his holy prophets" (Acts
> 3:19-21).

Yes, the Messiah already has come, but there is an aspect of the Messiah
and the age of the Messiah that has yet to be fully realized. Universal restoration
means a time of complete justice and right, truth and peace, love and faithfulness,
security and prosperity for all - the fullness of the messianic age. In Peter's
sermon, the coming of such restoration involves repentance.

Both Jews and Christians share that vision. But for my community and me
that messianic age already has begun. Jesus' ministry already let it break into our
lives with healing and restoring power - restoring us to our true relationship with
God and one another. He called us to live that future vision already. Just as the
future hope of resurrection already had happened in Jesus, so also Christians are
called to live that future vision of restoration, of justice and peace and joy, now.

With Jesus as history's lens, my community and I could look back to the
beginning of God's good creation and forward to its universal restoration. Jesus

fulfilled God's promises in the past and gave us a foretaste of God's promises for the future.

History and the Holy Spirit

For me, God's Spirit is at work in human history from beginning to end.[2] I had three major foci in my understanding of the work of God's Spirit: the time of Jesus; the time of Israel before Jesus, back to creation; the time of the church after Jesus, forward to the end of time. Let me deal with them chronologically.

The Hebrew scriptures witness to God's Spirit at work in Israel and beyond. Jesus himself points to the Spirit in Israel when he quotes from the prophet Isaiah (Lk. 4:18-19), but he also points beyond Israel to God at work in Sidon and Syria (Lk. 4:25-27). This period of time runs from creation through Israel's history up to and including John the Baptist.

> "The law and the prophets were in effect until John; since then the good
> news of the kingdom of God is proclaimed" (Lk. 16:16; note also Lk.
> 7:28).

The second focus is the work of the Spirit in the time of Jesus and his ministry. He is himself the "good news." Empowered by the Spirit at his baptism (Lk. 3:21-22), he affirms that the Spirit is upon him for his mission (Lk. 4:18-21). In *Luke* I tell of the Holy Spirit at work in Jesus.

The third focus is the work of the Spirit in the time of the Church and its ministry to the "end of the earth" and the end of time. It begins with the empowering of Jesus' followers at Pentecost. *Acts* is my story of the beginning of that time.

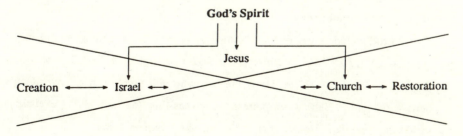

I do see myself as something of an "historian," not that I simply chronicle facts and figures, but that I *interpret* history in terms of God's Spirit at work in it. This means that I have a theology of history, a *theos logos* - "God understanding" of history - history as the time and place in which God is at work.

My community was part of the third period. I wanted them to see that God's Spirit was still working in them after the ending of *Acts*. I also wanted them to see that they were part of a much longer story in which God was at work in Israel, in Jesus, in the early church. As in the story of Pentecost, I wanted them to see that now the Spirit was poured out on them, their sons and daughters, to witness for God, see visions, and dream dreams for the sake of the good news in our time.

Jesus' final coming and history's end

First generation followers of Jesus expected his final coming and history's end in their lifetime. I wrote near the end of the second generation, so it clearly did not occur as expected. We had to come to grips with that disappointed expectation.

As I wrote earlier, even Mark, on the edge between the generations, may have given up on the timing of the end. Though God knows when the end will come, he indicates that Jesus didn't (Mk. 13:32; note also Mk. 13:3-7,21-22). So if Jesus had no timetable, neither should they.

We gave it no timetable either, but what were we to do? I wanted to turn the problem into an opportunity. Why a continuing history? I saw it as "an opportunity to testify" (Lk. 21:13; note also Mk. 13:10) and further the mission of good news to all people.

I did include much of Mark's imagery of Jesus' final coming and history's end (Lk. 21; 17:22-34).[3] The imagery includes the figure of the "Son of Man" (Lk. 17:22-25,30; 21:27,36). He is the one who will come to reign over God's new world. In the Hebrew scriptures, Daniel has this "apocalyptic" (revelatory) vision of "one like a son of man," that is, like a human being.

> "As I watched in the night visions, I saw one like a *son of man*, coming with the clouds of heaven. And he came to the Ancient One and was presented before him. To him was given dominion and glory and kingship, that all peoples, nations, and languages should serve him. His dominion is an ever-lasting dominion that shall not pass away, and his kingship is one that shall never be destroyed" (Dan. 7:13-14).

Early Christians applied that vision to Jesus' future coming.

> "Then they will see 'the Son of Man coming in a cloud' with great power and glory" (Lk. 21:27).

I too expect that future coming, but my community and I no longer expected it soon. However, let me say that I do retain texts from Mark which still could be interpreted this way.[4]

I did differ from Mark in how I saw the relationship of Jesus' future coming to the destruction of Jerusalem and the temple. Mark appears to join them closely together (Mk. 13:24). I wrote well after that destruction, refer to it with explicit detail (Lk. 21:20,24), and separate it from the Son of Man's coming. How could I do otherwise? The one already had happened; the other had yet to come. And, in Jesus' words, I had to warn my community not to go after false expectations of the end.

> "Then he said to the disciples, 'The days are coming when you will long to see one of the days of the Son of Man, and you will not see it. They will say to you, "Look there!" or "Look here!" Do not go, do not set off in pursuit'" (Lk. 17:22-23).

We had to live in a continuing history. It was "an opportunity to testify," even in the midst of persecution (Lk. 21:12-15). It was a time, not for lamenting the delay in Jesus' coming but for entering into our mission. I brought these words of Jesus to my community for our continuing journey.

> "Be on guard so that your hearts are not weighted down with dissipation and the worries of this life, and that day catch you unexpectedly, like a trap. For it will come upon all who live on the face of the earth. Be alert at all times, praying that you may have the strength to escape these things that will take place, and to stand before the Son of Man" (Lk. 21:34-36).

Jesus was and is that Son of Man - it is one of his titles. We now turn to it and other major titles from Hebrew history.

Titles for Jesus from Hebrew History

The titles that Jesus came to bear all had a prior history, most of them in Hebrew history. Applied to Jesus, they helped to illuminate him and his mission, for each of them had its own particular meaning. Though there are others (such as Savior, Teacher, King), I shall focus on four that occur many times in my writings.

Son of God

This title has its roots primarily in Israel's history (though other cultural backgrounds include it too). In the witness of the Hebrew scriptures, Israel is God's son.

"Thus says the Lord, 'Israel is my firstborn son'" (Ex. 4:22).

"When Israel was a child, I loved him, and out of Egypt I called my son" (Hos. 11:1).

For us, titles applied earlier to Israel, now apply to Jesus.

In *Luke*, the infancy stories (Lk. 1-2) declare that Jesus will be called "Son of God" (Lk. 1:35). In his baptism, "a voice came from heaven, 'You are my Son'" (Lk. 3:22; also 9:35). His genealogy goes back to Adam, "son of God" (Lk. 3:38). Even the devil and the demons refer to him as Son of God (Lk. 4:3,9,41; 8:28).

However, in *Luke*, Jesus never refers to himself as Son of God, though religious leaders, seeking charges against him, interpret Jesus as doing so.

"All of them asked, 'Are you, then, the Son of God?' He said to them, 'You say that I am.' Then they said, 'What further testimony do we need? We have heard it from his own lips!'" (Lk. 22:70-71).

In *Acts*, Paul proclaims Jesus as Son of God (Acts 9:20). Words of a psalm, applied earlier to Israel's king, he now applies to Jesus.

"You are my Son; today I have begotten you" (Acts 13:33 from Ps. 2:7).

Early Christians reached back into their past Hebrew heritage to let Israel's title as Son of God now serve to proclaim Jesus.

The texts from *Exodus* and *Hosea* above focus on "son" language in relationship to Israel's liberation from Egyptian bondage. For me, Jesus as Son of God proclaims primarily God's liberating work. Baptized and empowered by the Spirit as God's Son, now Jesus is "to let the oppressed go free" (Lk. 4:19). Now Jesus as God's Son frees people from demonic power (Lk. 8:28-29).

Son of Man

This title (referred to in the previous section) also comes from Israel's heritage. However, whereas "Son of God" focuses on Israel *in the past*, "Son of Man" focuses on a figure *in the future* (as shown in the earlier quotation from Daniel).[5] Son of Man (meaning "human being") was the title applied to that human-like figure who would come in the future to judge earth's peoples and bring God's new world. Jesus himself spoke of the Son of Man; and early Christians drew that future figure into the present and applied it to Jesus.

In *Luke*, Jesus always refers to the Son of Man in the third person (some 25 times), and only he uses it (except Lk. 24:7; Acts 7:56, *Acts'* only use of the title).[6] Did he in his ministry refer to himself as the Son of Man?

It is clear that, after his death and resurrection, we saw Jesus as that Son of Man who would bring God's new world. But is it possible that Jesus may have considered the Son of Man a future figure other than himself? If that were true, then he may have understood his ministry as a call to respond to God's reign and get ready for the Son of Man's coming.

However, as the first generation of Christians passed without the Son of Man's coming, then early Christians reshaped the story to identify Jesus with the

Son of Man yet to come,[7] as well as to apply that future title to Jesus in his earthly life. Jesus was that human being, that Son of Man.

For them, Jesus was not only the *coming* Son of Man. He already was the Son of Man in his suffering, death, resurrection, and exaltation.[8] He already was the Son of Man in his ministry.[9]

So the title, Son of Man, ties the future and the present together in Jesus. The one who shall reign over God's new world in the future already has been here to forgive sins (Lk. 5:24); to seek and save the lost (Lk. 19:10); to suffer, die, and be raised - all to bring good news of great joy for all the people.

Messiah (Christ)

This title also has its roots in Israel's life. *Messiah* comes directly from the Hebrew, *Christ* from its Greek form. The term means "anointed one." The noun occurs some 10 times in *Luke* and 15 times in *Acts*, the verb "to anoint" once in *Luke* and twice in *Acts*.[10]

In Israel's life, they anointed kings, including the most important of all, David. Later expectations for a Messiah were linked to David's line with hope of restoring Israel again to heights of political and military power as in his time.[11]

Jesus and early Christians had to challenge such an understanding. When Peter confesses Jesus as God's Messiah (Lk. 9:20), Jesus charges them not to tell anyone. People then could interpret it too easily in terms of political and military power. Jesus interpreted it in terms of rejection, death, and resurrection (Lk. 9:21-22), of suffering and glory (Lk. 24:26), of suffering and resurrection (Lk. 24:46).

Jesus called on David in the *Psalms* to answer No to the question, Is the Messiah David's son? (Lk.20:41-44). When religious leaders ask Jesus if he were the Messiah, Jesus responds by turning to the title, Son of Man (Lk. 22:67-69). And when they accuse Jesus of proclaiming himself as "the Messiah, a king," the Roman governor Pilate finds no basis for it (Lk. 23:22-24).

It is clear in *Luke* that Jesus *is* the Messiah, but he rarely if ever refers to himself as such. However, others proclaim him as the Messiah. The angelic messenger proclaims him "a Savior, who is the Messiah, the Lord" (Lk. 2:11). Simeon speaks of having seen "the Lord's Messiah" (Lk. 2:26). The demons know that he is the Messiah (Lk. 4:41). Peter confesses him as "the Messiah of God" (Lk. 9:20).

In *Acts*, Peter proclaims the crucified and risen Jesus as Lord and Messiah (Acts 2:31-36, with support from David). He says that the Messiah would suffer (Acts 3:18), that God would send the Messiah (Acts 3:20), and that the Messiah would face opposition (Acts 4:25-27). The apostles and Philip teach and proclaim Jesus as the Messiah (Acts 5:42; 8:5,12). Peter credits healing to Jesus Christ (Acts 9:34) and speaks to the Roman officer Cornelius of "peace by Jesus Christ" (Acts 10:36). Paul argues that the suffering and risen Jesus is indeed the Messiah: in Damascus (Acts 9:22), in Thessalonica (17:3), in Corinth (18:5), in Jerusalem (26:23).

These examples from my story show how important it was to proclaim Jesus as God's Messiah. It did call for interpreting him, not as a powerful political and military messiah, but as a suffering, crucified, and risen Messiah who saved others and did not save himself. He was not a messiah whose followers Rome needed to crush. He was a Messiah whose followers, like us, wanted to bring good news and peace for all in the Empire.

Lord (Kurios)

This title is more confusing than the others because I use it in referring to both the God of Israel and Jesus. I use it about 80 times each in *Luke* and *Acts*. About two thirds refer to God, one third to Jesus.[12]

The Hebrew scriptures refer often to God as *Lord*, and my infancy stories use it this way nearly 20 times. For example, Zechariah sings

"Blessed be the Lord God of Israel, for he has looked favorably on his people and redeemed them" (Lk. 1:68).

As early Christian saw the Lord God of Israel at work in Jesus, they transferred the title *Lord* to Jesus. God's reign and lordship now focused in him. As Peter proclaimed,

"Therefore let the entire house of Israel know with certainty that God has made him both Lord and Messiah" (Acts 2:36).

Here I shall limit my discussion to those places where I refer to *Jesus* as Lord. However, that they are a third of my total use shows how important it is to remember that two thirds refer to God. It is God the Lord who is at work in Jesus as Lord.

In the infancy stories Elizabeth speaks of "the mother of my Lord" (Lk. 1:43), and God's messenger proclaims to the shepherds, "to you is born this day in the city of David a Savior, who is the Messiah, the Lord" (Lk. 2:11).

In *Luke* many address Jesus as Lord: Peter (Lk. 5:8; 22:33), a leper (5:12), a Roman officer (7:6), a follower (9:61), the disciples (9:54,59; 10:17; 11:1; 17:37; 22:49; Acts 1:6), a blind man (18:41), tax collector Zacchaeus (19:8), David (20:42,44; also Acts 2:25-28,34-35), others (13:23,25).

I refer to Jesus as Lord when he sees the widow at Nain (7:13), appoints the seventy (10:1), speaks to a Pharisee (11:39) and to a synagogue ruler (13:15); when the apostles speak to him and he to them (17:5-6) and Jesus speaks to a pleading widow (18:6).

Jesus himself also uses the term.

"And he said to them, 'The Son of Man is lord of the sabbath'" (Lk. 6:5)

"Why do you call me 'Lord, Lord,' and do not do what I tell you?" (Lk. 6:46).

"If anyone asks you, 'why are you untying it (a colt)?' just say this, 'The Lord needs it'" (Lk. 19:31).

In the last chapter, Jesus' disciples proclaim, "The Lord has risen indeed" (Lk. 24:34).

Jesus' resurrection really provides the basis for proclaiming Jesus as Lord (note Acts 2:31-36). Through the lens of the resurrection we early Christians could see him as Lord also from his birth through his baptism and ministry and death. "This Jesus God raised up. . . God has made him both Lord and Messiah (Acts 2:32,34). From the end backwards we could see him as Lord in his entire life and ministry.

Acts uses Lord about as many times as *Luke*, again with about two thirds referring to God and one third to Jesus. I shall touch on only the latter.

One phrase that occurs in *Acts* but not in *Luke* is "the Lord Jesus." The apostles give testimony "to the resurrection of the Lord Jesus" (Acts 4:33). At his stoning, Stephen prayed, "Lord Jesus, receive my spirit" (Acts 7:59; note Lk. 23:46).[13] Paul and Silas respond to the jailer, "Believe in the Lord Jesus" (Acts 16:31).[14] Paul is willing to die "for the name of the Lord Jesus" (Acts 21:13).

In the *Acts* story, people are added to or brought to or believe in the Lord (Acts 5:14; 9:42; 11:24; 18:8), walk in the fear of the Lord (9:31), turn to the Lord (9:35), are faithful to the Lord (11:23; 16:15).

Acts speaks of remembering the word of the Lord (11:16), being astonished at the teaching of the Lord (13:12), speaking boldly for the Lord (14:3), being entrusted to the Lord (14:23), "serving the Lord with all humility and with tears, enduring the trials" (20:19).

In some places the Lord speaks to persons in visions and they respond: Paul on the Damascus Road (9:4-6; 22:7-10; 26:14-18); Ananias in Damascus (9:10-16); Paul in Corinth:

> "One night the Lord said to Paul in a vision, 'Do not be afraid, but speak
> and do not be silent; for I am with you, and no one will lay a hand on
> you to harm you, for there are many in this city who are my people'"
> (Acts 18:9-10).

The Lord speaks to Paul in Jerusalem during temple prayer (Acts 22:17-21). He speaks in the night:

''That night the Lord stood by him (Paul) and said, 'Keep up your courage! For just as you have testified for me in Jerusalem, so you must bear witness also in Rome''' (23:11).

The visions are not an end in themselves. They serve the cause of the Christian mission to ''bring salvation to the ends of the earth'' (Acts 13:47).

All the major titles Jesus bears have their roots in past history. That past history illuminated the present and pointed the way into the future for me and my community. It is a future to bring ''universal restoration.'' It will bring God's full measure of love and justice, truth and health, peace and joy, for all who want to share in God's inclusive, beloved human family.

Jesus already embodied that vision in his ministry. Now that vision falls to those who follow him - to seek to live that vision in the present as we move toward God's new world in the future.

We already have written about the Holy Spirit in this chapter. This is so important in *Luke-Acts* that I devote the entire next conversation to the work of the Holy Spirit.

Endnotes

[1]For Luke, Jesus himself is something of an Elijah figure who precedes the final coming of the Messiah. Luke omits references to Elijah three times where Mark and Matthew have them (Mt. 11:14; 17:12; Mk. 9:13; Mt. 27:47-49; Mk. 15:35-36). They identify Elijah with John the Baptist. Luke does refer to Elijah in Lk. 9:8,19,30,33; note too Lk. 1:17; 4:25-26.

[2]In terms of the beginning and ending of the way our Bibles are put together, God's wind or spirit is at work in the first chapter of Genesis (Gen. 1:2) and the last chapter of Revelation (Rev. 22:17).

[3]The imagery of Mark 13 had its roots in Jewish apocalyptic writings like Daniel 7:9-14. "Apocalyptic" comes from the Greek word having to do with "revealing," here of the future.

[4]Mk. 9:1, Lk. 9:27; Mk. 13:30, Lk. 21:32.

[5]Some scholars see "Son of Man" as meaning simply "human being." One finds some basis for this in Ezekiel. However, that understanding fails to do justice to the many references directed to the future.

[6]When others confront Jesus with the title Messiah, he shifts the talk to Son of Man (Lk. 9:20-22; 22:67-69).

[7]See Lk. 9:26; 12:8,40; 17:22,24,26,30; 18:8; 21:27,36.

[8]See Lk. 9:22,44; 18:31; 22:22,48; 24:7; 22:69; Acts 7:56.

[9]See Lk. 5:24; 6:5; 9:58; 11:30; 19:10.

[10]Lk. 4:18; Acts 4:27; 10:38.

[11]See Lk. 1:32-33,68-69; 2:11; 24:21; Acts 1:6.

[12]A few uses refer to neither and are translated "master" or "sir."

[13]Like Jesus in Luke (Lk. 23:34), Stephen also prays for those who kill him (Acts 7:60).

[14]See also Acts 9:17; 11:17; 20:21,24,35; 28:31.

CHAPTER 6

My Understanding of the Holy Spirit

"God anointed Jesus of Nazareth with the Holy Spirit and with power;
and he went about doing good and healing all who were oppressed by the
devil, for God was with him" (Acts 10:38).

"You will receive power when the Holy Spirit has come upon you and you will
be my witnesses in Jerusalem, in all Judea and Samaria, and to the ends of the
earth" (Acts 1:8).

God's power for a purpose

My primary understanding of the Holy Spirit is the presence of God's
power, God's energy, to accomplish a purpose. The possible translations of
pneuma (spirit) also as "wind" and "breath" point to the life-giving force of that
Spirit; and the understanding of "holy" as "whole" (God's holiness is God's
wholeness, integrity) points to the whole-making, healing, health-bringing work
of that Spirit. The texts quoted above proclaim that life-giving, whole-making
power in the missions of both Jesus and his followers.

When I speak of God, I point to the Creator - the "living God who made
the heaven and the earth" (Acts 14:15), the "Sovereign Lord, who made the
heaven and earth, the sea, and everything in them" (Acts 4:24). My genealogy of

Jesus goes back to God the Creator (Lk. 3:38), and it is the Holy Spirit of the Creator who is at work in Jesus' conception. God's messenger says to Mary:

"The Holy Spirit will come upon you, and the power of the Most High will overshadow you; therefore the child to be born will be holy, he will be called Son of God" (Lk. 1:35).

I did not want simply to tell of the start of the work of God's Holy Spirit in Jesus at his baptism. I wanted to show God's life-giving purpose at work in Jesus from his birth.

To speak of the Holy Spirit is to speak of God's purpose of "doing good and healing" in this world. That purpose has been expansively at work from the beginning of human history.

An expanding purpose

I understand God to be at work in nature, as well as in human history (see Lk. 12:24-28). However (as indicated already in the last chapter), I focus my use of "Spirit" language in three places: in Israel, in Jesus, and in the early church. The *Hebrew Scriptures* witness to the first, *Luke* to the second, and *Acts* to the third. Here I need to say a word about the terms I use.

The *Hebrew Scriptures* rarely refer to the *Holy* Spirit but simply to the Spirit. However, in my writings, whether I use Holy Spirit or Spirit, I refer to God the Holy One's Spirit at work. I also mean that same Spirit when I refer to "the Spirit of Jesus" (see Acts 16:6-7).

My direct references to the Spirit expand in the course of my writings. I refer to the Spirit in the Hebrew scriptures and in the Infancy Stories (Lk. 1-2) only a half dozen times each. I refer to the Spirit at work in Jesus' ministry about ten times, though I understand his entire ministry as empowered by the Spirit. I refer to the Spirit at work in the church in *Acts* some fifty five times. It is clear that my *direct* use of "Spirit" falls heavily on God's expanding missionary purpose.

In my *direct* references the Spirit at work in Israel I see the Spirit at work in Elijah (Lk. 1:17), in Isaiah (Lk. 4:18-19; Acts 28:25-27), in Joel (Acts 2:17,33), in David (Acts 1:16; 4:25).

The Infancy Stories promise that John the Baptist "will be filled with the Holy Spirit" for his preparatory mission (Lk. 1:15-17).[1] John's mother Elizabeth also is "filled with the Holy Spirit" in her proclaiming a blessing on Mary and the pre-natal Jesus (Lk. 1:41-45), as is John's father Zechariah in his prophecy of God's saving deed of mercy in Jesus (Lk. 1:67-79). The Spirit is at work in Jesus' conception (Lk. 1:35); and the Spirit reveals knowledge to Simeon and guides him (Lk. 2:25-32).

The sections that follow will develop the work of the Spirit in Jesus' ministry and in the church's mission.

Power for Jesus' mission

For me, the single most important work of the Holy Spirit is to empower people for mission: Jesus in his time; the early church in its time; my community in our time. The Spirit empowered Jesus at his baptism.

> "the Holy Spirit descended upon him in bodily form like a dove. And a voice came from heaven, 'You are my Son, the Beloved; *in you I-have-willed-the-good*" (Lk. 3:22, underlined, my translation).

The Spirit empowered Jesus to do God's good will in the world. My words, "in bodily form," emphasize that the Spirit is not some vague vision, but God's particular and real power concretely at work in Jesus' mission.

I tell how Jesus spells out what that mission involves by his reading from and pointing to the fulfillment of the prophet Isaiah.

> "The Spirit of the Lord is upon me, . . . has anointed me to bring good news to the poor . . . sent me to proclaim release to the captives and recovery of sight to the blind, to let the oppressed go free, to proclaim the year of the Lord's favor" (Lk. 4:18-19).

Much of the rest of *Luke* unfolds that Spirit-empowered purpose in Jesus' ministry: in his teaching, preaching, healing. God's Spirit empowers people, not simply for private inspiration but for public action that can mean good news to the poor, the captives, the blind, the oppressed.

Before Jesus began his mission, "filled with the power of the Spirit" (Lk. 4:14), he had to face temptation. Yet "full of the Spirit" and "led by the Spirit" (Lk. 4:1), he faced temptation by evil power victoriously.

Later, in his Spirit-empowered ministry Jesus faced victoriously the evil or unclean spirits that held people captive (Lk. 6:36).[2] Jesus as one in whom God's *good* Spirit was at work to heal had to challenge the *bad* spirits (the word *pneuma* is the same for both) at work to destroy. Jesus had to face and overcome evil that enslaved and thwarted people's lives as God's beloved children, be that evil physical or psychic, religious or political, private or public, economic or social.

I wanted the Spirit to empower my community also to battle such enslaving evil and be God's agents of freeing good will for all people. I wanted them to "rejoice in the Holy Spirit" for God's opening a message to children (Lk. 10:21). I wanted them to know that they could ask God to give them the Holy Spirit (Lk. 11:13), though such asking was not for their private enjoyment but for the sake of entering into Jesus' liberating mission (Lk. 11:14-23). I wanted to assure them that the Spirit would enable them to face and speak to their persecutors.

> "When they bring you before the synagogues, the rulers, and the authorities, do not worry about how you are to defend yourselves or what you are to say; for the Holy Spirit will teach you at that very hour what you ought to say" (Lk. 12:12).

That Spirit was with Jesus as he faced persecution and death. In death Jesus commended his spirit, God's breath and life in him, to God (Lk. 23:46).[3] In both life and death, Jesus and we ourselves belong to the breathing, empowering God of life.

Power on the move

The power of the Spirit moves. Past promises are fulfilled, but once fulfilled they become new promises. For instance, the Spirit was at work in Isaiah in his time, "The Spirit of the Lord is upon me..." (Is. 61:1-2). Then Jesus read that text and applied it to himself, fulfilling Isaiah in a new way (Lk. 4:18- 21). In turn, the Spirit at work in Jesus will move on to be at work in his followers.

John the Baptist promises that "one more powerful than I is coming...He will baptize you with the Holy Spirit and fire" (Lk. 3:16). Jesus proclaims that promise in both *Luke* and *Acts*.

> "And see, I am sending upon you what my Father promised; so stay here in the city until you have been clothed with power from on high" (Lk. 24:49; note Acts 1:2).

> "While staying with them, he ordered them not to leave Jerusalem, but to wait there for the promise of the Father. 'This,' he said, 'is what you have heard from me; for John baptized with water, but you will be baptized with the Holy Spirit not many days from now'" (Acts 1:5; note Acts 11:16).

The coming of the Spirit upon them at Pentecost fulfills that promise, "All of them were filled with the Holy Spirit" (Acts 2:4). A voice from the Hebrew past joins in this fulfillment in Peter's proclamation.

> "this is what was spoken by the prophet Joel, 'In the last days it will be, God, declares, that I will pour out my Spirit upon all flesh, and your sons and daughters shall prophesy, and your young men shall see visions, and your old men dream dreams. Even upon my slaves, both men and women, in those days I will pour out my Spirit; and they shall prophesy'" (Acts 2:16-18; note also vs. 33).

And Pentecost was only the beginning of that new outpouring for the sake of a mission "to the ends of the earth."

We cannot limit the work of God's Spirit to one period of human history. That Spirit is at work in Isaiah and Joel, in Jesus, at Pentecost, and beyond. Past promises fulfilled become new promises to further the mission of God's good news. I wanted my community to understand that now that moving power of the Holy Spirit would be at work in them too.

Power for mission among Jews

Like Jesus himself, all of his first followers were Jews. They were the ones baptized by the Spirit at Pentecost for their mission, just as Jesus was baptized by the Spirit for his mission. Their mission was to begin in Jerusalem and Judea (Acts 1:8) and focus first on their own people. Peter proclaimed to them,

> "Repent, and be baptized everyone of you in the name of the Lord Jesus so that your sins may be forgiven; and you will receive the gift of the Holy Spirit. For the promise is for you, for your children, and for all who are far away, everyone whom the Lord our God calls to him" (Acts 2:38-39; note also 5:30-32).

Incidentally, I understood the basic sequence in Christian preaching to be: 1) proclaiming Jesus as Lord and Messiah, 2) calling for repentance ("mind-change"), 3) baptism in the name of Jesus[4] with forgiveness ("letting go" the past), and 4) promise of the Spirit to empower for mission. However (as we shall see later), this is not always the sequence. We cannot control God and confine the work of the Holy Spirit to any inflexible, institutional patterns. God's Spirit is free.

The mission among Jews involved meeting the challenge by their religious leaders. Peter, "filled by the Holy Spirit," has to defend his healing of a lame man "by the name of Jesus Christ of Nazareth" (Acts 4:5-10). The Spirit empowers those who must meet and speak to challenges (note again Lk. 12:11-12). I did not want my community to think that their Spirit-powered mission would be an easy, obstacle-free task, but I wanted to assure them that the Holy Spirit would be with them, come what may.[5]

Power for mission among Samaritans

The mission also reached out to Samaritans (Acts 1:8). Samaritans were the heirs of those Jews who had intermarried with non-Jews after the exile in Babylon. Though they had the same scriptures, they were despised as heretics by Jews and established their own center of worship and religious practices. As with other outcasts, I lift up my special concern for them and present them in a very positive light in *Luke* (Lk. 10:30-37; 17:11-19).

As I tell the story in *Acts*, Philip proclaimed the Messiah to the Samaritans with good response (Acts 8:5-8). Hearing this, Peter and John went to Samaria to pray for them,

> "that they might receive the Holy Spirit (for as yet the Spirit had not come upon any of them; they had only been baptized in the name of the Lord Jesus). Then Peter and John laid their hands upon them, and they received the Holy Spirit" (Acts 8:15-16).

To be baptized "in Jesus' name" means to *enter into* all that he stands for as God's gift of good news. To receive the Holy Spirit is to know God's power to *go out* and share that good news with others. In baptism, God's presence in Jesus reaches out to embrace us. In receiving the Holy Spirit, God's power enables us to reach out and embrace others with God's good news. The laying on of hands makes the flow of the Spirit from one person to another very specific, sharing God's gift of power with others so they in turn can pass it on. This is what Peter and John did.

Philip not only proclaimed Jesus to the Samaritans. The Spirit also directed him to speak to and baptize an Ethiopian court official who was a eunuch (Acts 8:26-38; it was not uncommon for such officials to be eunuchs)[6] and to preach in that region (vss. 39-40). The Spirit-empowered mission kept expanding and

> "the church throughout Judea, Galilee, and Samaria had peace and was built up. Living in the fear of the Lord and in the comfort of the Holy Spirit, it increased in numbers" (Acts 9:31; note also 13:52).

I wanted that expanding mission in the power of the Spirit then to serve as a model for an expanding mission in my time.

Power for mission among Gentiles

Both Saul/Paul of Tarsus (as a Jew living in a Greek context, he had two names; Saul was his Hebrew name, Paul his Greek name) and Peter play crucial roles in opening the mission to the non-Jewish Gentiles. After Paul's transformation from being a persecutor of Christians to being God's instrument "to bring my name before Gentiles and kings and before the people of Israel" (Acts 9:15), Ananias spoke to him of being "filled with the Holy Spirit" (Acts 9:17) for that mission.

As to Peter, after his "breakthrough" vision (Acts 10:9-16), the Spirit directed him to the Gentile Cornelius (vss. 19-29; 11:12) and Peter proclaimed,

> "I truly understand that God shows no partiality, but in every nation
> anyone who fears him and does what it is right is acceptable to him"
> (Acts 10:34-35).

However, here is a change in sequence from what we saw earlier, not from baptism to the gift of the Spirit but the reverse.

> "While Peter was still speaking, the Holy Spirit fell upon all who heard
> the word. The circumcised (Jewish) believers who had come with Peter
> were astounded that the gift of the Holy Spirit had been poured out even
> on the Gentiles, for they heard them speaking in tongues and extolling
> God. Then Peter said, 'Can anyone withhold the water for baptizing these
> people who have received the Holy Spirit just as we have?' So he ordered
> them to be baptized in the name of Jesus Christ" (Acts 10:44-48; see also
> 11:15-18; 15:8-9).

The sequence is not of primary importance. The essential elements are: word, Spirit, baptism. Here the main point is that "the gift of the Holy Spirit had been poured out even on Gentiles."

The mission to the Gentiles continued from Antioch where

> "the Holy Spirit said, 'Set apart for me Barnabas and Saul for the word to which I have called them'" (Acts 13:2; note also vs. 4. Barnabas was "a good man, full of the Holy Spirit and faith," Acts 11:24).

Part of that mission for Paul, "filled with the Holy Spirit," was to challenge false prophets and crooks (Acts 13:6-11; note also liars, Acts 5:3,5).

I tell also of an important meeting of earliest Christians to sort out some perspectives on the Gentile mission. It was to determine how many Jewish customs Gentile Christians needed to observe in order to accommodate their Jewish Christian sisters and brothers. There was no question that God had indeed given the Holy Spirit to the Gentiles (Acts 15:8). They decided to send a letter to the Gentile Christians in Antioch, saying,

> "it has seemed good to the Holy Spirit and to us to impose on you no further burden than these essentials: that you abstain from what has been sacrificed to idols and from blood and from what is strangled and from fornication. If you keep yourselves from these, you will do well. Farewell" (Acts 15:28-29).

I told this to emphasize the unity among earliest Christians - how the Spirit helped them to work out their problems for the sake of a mission that could include both Jews and Gentiles. In the mission to the Gentiles, the Spirit also directed Paul and Timothy where *not* to go (Acts 16:6-7), as well as where to go (Acts 19:21).

I tell also of a striking event that occurred in Ephesus. There Paul said to Jesus' followers,

> "'Did you receive the Holy Spirit when you became believers?' And they said, 'No, we have not even heard that there is a Holy Spirit.' Then he said, 'Into what then were you baptized?' They answered, 'Into John's baptism.' Paul said, John baptized with the baptism of repentance, telling people to believe in the one who was to come after him, that is, in Jesus.' On hearing this, they were baptized in the name of the Lord Jesus. When Paul had laid his hands upon them the Holy Spirit came upon them, and they spoke in tongues and prophesied" (Acts 19:2-7).

As I noted earlier, in my time there still were some people who thought that John the Baptist was the Messiah. My telling of the event in Ephesus could help them not to confuse Jesus and John and to see that Jesus truly is the Messiah.

Here we see again the pattern of baptism in the name of Jesus coupled with empowerment by the Spirit. The two belong together: identifying with Jesus and empowering by the Spirit. I wanted to emphasize this for my community too.

A final note on Paul and the Spirit

With his work in the northeastern area of the Mediterranean world completed, the Spirit guided him further.

> "Paul resolved in the Spirit to go through Macedonia and Achaia, and then to go on to Jerusalem. He said, 'After I have been there, I must also see Rome" (Acts 19:21).

Yet he also confessed, the Spirit revealed that trouble awaited him.

> "And now, as a captive to the Spirit, I am on my way to Jerusalem, not knowing what will happen to me there, except that the Holy Spirit testifies to me in every city that imprisonments and persecutions are waiting for me. But I do not count my life of any value to myself, if only I may finish my course and the ministry that I received from the Lord Jesus, to testify to the good news of God's grace" (Acts 20: 22-24).

For my community to listen to these words from Paul would help them to be faithful in their ministry, whatever persecution might await them.

In his Spirit-led journey, even knowing persecution awaited him, Paul still cared about the churches he had founded. He said to the elders at Ephesus:

> "Keep watch over yourselves and over the flock, of which the Holy Spirit has made you overseers, to shepherd the church of God that he obtained with the blood of his own son. I know that after I have gone, savage wolves will come in among you, not sparing the flock. Some even from your own group will come distorting the truth in order to entice disciples to follow them . . . And now I commend you to God and the message of his grace, a message that is able to build you up and give you an inheritance among all who are sanctified" (Acts 20:28-32).

It was a word my community needed to hear also. We needed to "shepherd the flock" and protect them from those who would distort the truth of God's gracious good news. My writing of *Luke- Acts* was part of proclaiming and defending the truth of that good news.

Some words of Paul here called for a bit of explanation. The words, "the blood of his own son" point to God's grace and love. Blood language is the language of life poured out in love for others. In Jesus' death, God shows how far his love for us will go, faithful even to death. That grace and love goes so far even for Jesus to pray for those who killed him, "Father, forgive them, for they do not know what they are doing" (Lk. 23:34).

The word "sanctified" has the same Greek root as the word "holy." The "sanctified" are the "holy ones," the "saints" (all from the same Greek root). They are not those who have reached moral perfection. They are those whose lives have been touched by the Holy Spirit and empowered to live out a mission that brings good news to the poor, the captive, the blind, the oppressed. That is the most important form of "spirituality" - the Holy Spirit at work in us to bring "good news of great joy to all people."

In *Luke*, Jesus relates that good news strongly to God's reign, God's kingdom. It is to that reign at work in him that we turn in our next conversation.

Endnotes

[1]Luke also links John to the Hebrew scriptures ("the law and the prophets," Lk. 16:16; see also Lk. 7:28).

[2]See also Lk. 6:18-19; 7:21; 8:1-2,29.

[3]This is one of three distinct words of Jesus from the cross in Luke (see Lk. 23:34,43 for the others). This word from the cross quotes Ps. 31:5. Assuming that Luke knew Mark's gospel, Luke may have had a problem with Mark's "My God, my God, why have you forsaken me" (Mk. 15:34 from Ps. 22:1). In any case, Luke omits this word from Mark and has instead the words from Ps. 31).

[4]This formula, "baptism in the name of Jesus," reveals that early Christians used more than one. We are most familiar in our liturgies with the form in Matthew, "in the name of the Father and of the Son and of the Holy Spirit" (Mt. 28:19). To recognize the diversity of early Christians, as expressed in New Testament writings, lends biblical support for continuing diversity in our churches today.

[5]It is those "full of the Spirit" who are chosen to assist the apostles (Acts 6:3,5). The martyr Stephen challenged those who "resist the Holy Spirit" (Acts 7:51) and spoke "full of the Holy Spirit" (Acts 7:55).

[6]The only other use of the term "eunuch" in the New Testament is in Matthew's Gospel. It includes a reference to those "who have made themselves eunuchs for the sake of the kingdom of heaven" (Mt. 19:12). The context points to not letting one's sexual desire interfere with one's commitment to God's reign.

CHAPETR 7

My Understanding of God's Reign in Jesus

"Soon afterwards he went on through cities and villages, proclaiming and bringing the kingdom (reign) of God" (Lk. 8:1).

God's reign in Jesus in the present

I relate "reign" ("kingdom") language to God or Jesus more than 40 times in *Luke-Acts*. Nothing seems clearer among early Christians than that Jesus himself proclaimed the presence of God's reign, of God at work to rule with outreaching and liberating compassion and good news for all people.

Yet that reign did not begin with Jesus. It has deep roots in Israel's understanding of God as king.[1] But now Israel's God reigns anew in Jesus' ministry. God's reign makes a new "visitation" (Lk. 1:68,78; 19:44. It "comes near" (Lk. 10:9,11). It is something people have longed for. Jesus says to his disciples,

> "Blessed are the eyes that see what you see! For I tell you that many prophets and kings desired to see what you see, but did not see it, and to hear what you hear, but did not hear it" (Lk. 10:23-24; see also Lk. 11:29-32; 16:16; 7:28).

God's reign is at work in Jesus and his ministry.

However, it is important to note that in *Luke-Acts* I refer to God's reign in terms both of its *presence* in Jesus and of its *future* in his final coming. Thus there is an *already* aspect, as well as a *not yet* aspect to God's reign. The focus in this section is on the present.

What does God's reign in Jesus do? In one instance, Jesus' opponents accuse him of casting out demons by the ruler of demons, Beelzebul (Lk. 11:14-23). But that doesn't make sense, for then Beelzebul would work against himself. Jesus declares,

> "But if it is by the finger of God that I cast out demons, then the kingdom of God has come upon you" (Lk. 11:20).

Among other things, the working of God's reign in Jesus means "to let the oppressed go free" (Lk. 4:19) - to free people from the many bondages that oppress them, be they physical, psychic, social, religious. Jesus preaching-teaching-healing ministry shows that God's reigning, liberating purpose is at work in the present in him.

Once asked when the reign of God was coming, Jesus answered,

> "The kingdom of God is not coming with things that can be observed; nor will they say, 'Look, here it is!' or 'There it is!'" For, in fact, the kingdom of God is among you" (Lk. 17:20-21; this translation is preferred to "within you").

God's reign was not simply something to wait for and observe in the future. It was at work already in Jesus' healing ministry. Jesus' healing of ten lepers precedes the quotation above.

How does one come to experience and know God's reign? How did Jesus' disciples come to know it? The following quotation about "secrets" may point to one answer.

> "Then his disciples asked him what this parable meant. He said, 'To you it has been given to know the secrets of the kingdom of God; but to others I speak in parables, so that "looking they may not perceive, and listening they may not understand"'" (Lk. 8:9-10; quotes Is. 6:9; see also Jer. 5:21; Ezek. 12:2; kingdom parables in Lk. 13:18-19,20-21).

What does such an understanding of parables intend?

Parables intend to confront the hearer with her/his own life, invite her/him to enter into the parable, and call for a decision. This means that one cannot perceive and understand a parable as a detached onlooker. One has to enter into it.

So, just as one understands love by loving, the disciples understood God's reign by entering into it as they followed Jesus, the one in whom that reign was at work. They no longer were detached onlookers. They understood the "secrets" of God's reign because they had risked entering into it and letting God's liberating reign in Jesus change their lives.

I wanted my community to know that the presence of God's reign in Jesus was not only something in the past for the first disciples. It was something for them to enter into now also and to know that God's liberating work in Jesus was still occurring.

God's reign in the future

My writings maintain a tension between God's reign already present in Jesus' ministry and the full realization of that reign in the future. God's reign of liberty and love, justice and joy, health and peace at work in Jesus as God's Messiah promises a future fullness. Early Christians proclaimed God's reign as both present and future.

We have seen that the first generation of Christians expected that future in their lifetime. Christians like I in the second and third generations had to release such expectation from any timetable,[2] but we did not give it up.

Here let me discuss a text in which I largely follow Mark's witness to words of Jesus (Mk. 8:38-9:1).

> "Those who are ashamed of me and of my words, of them the Son of Man will be ashamed when he comes in his glory and the glory of the Father and the holy angels. But truly I tell you, there are some standing here who will not taste death before they see the kingdom of God" (Lk. 9:26-27).

One might interpret this text as identifying the coming Son of Man with the kingdom of God. However, I would separate them and point to those in the first generation who did see the kingdom of God in Jesus (note the texts quoted earlier that follow, Lk. 10:23-24; Lk. 11:20). So in my understanding, this text contains the tension between Jesus' future coming as the Son of Man and God's reign already at work in him.

I interpret the following witnesses to Jesus' words also as maintaining that tension.

> ''Then they will see 'the Son of Man coming in a cloud' with great power and glory. Now when you see these things begin to take place, stand up and raise your heads, because your redemption is drawing near. Then he told them a parable: 'Look at the fig tree and all the leaves; as soon as they sprout leaves you can see for yourselves and know that summer is already near. So also, when you see these things taking place, you know that the kingdom of God is near. Truly I tell you, this generation will not pass away until all things have taken place''' (Lk. 21:27-32).

Again, one could interpret this text as identifying the Son of Man's future coming and the kingdom of God. However, I do not limit the coming of great power to the future Son of Man. The first generation did not pass away until it had seen that power, not only in Jesus' ministry (Lk. 4:14,36) but also in the mission of his first followers.

> ''So when they had come together, they asked him, 'Lord, is this the time when you will restore the kingdom to Israel?' He replied, 'It is not for you to know the times or periods that the Father has set by his own authority. But you will receive power when the Holy Spirit has come upon you; and you will be my witnesses''' (Acts 1:6-8).

Great power will come in the future coming of the Son of Man, but that power is not only future. It is present too in the power of Jesus' ministry and in the empowered witness of the earliest Christians. My community lived at a time between the two - between the power at work in Jesus in the past and his power yet to come in the future. Now Jesus was calling us to be his empowered community of witness in our time.

Eating and drinking in the future

Some texts do point distinctively to a future fulfillment beyond human history. One occurs in my telling of Jesus' words at the Last Supper.[3]

> "He said to them, 'I have eagerly desired to eat this Passover with you before I suffer; for I tell you, I will not eat of it until it is fulfilled in the kingdom of God.' Then he took a cup, and after giving thanks he said, 'Take this and divide it among yourselves; for I tell you that from now on I will not drink of the fruit of the vine until the kingdom of God comes'" (Lk. 22:15-18)

Jesus ate and drank with people during his ministry (even got into trouble for doing so, Lk., 7:34). He ate and drank with his disciples at the Last Supper. He will eat and drink at the "messianic banquet" beyond history in the fullness of God's reign.

> "You are those who have stood by me in my trials; and I confer on you, just as my Father conferred on me, a kingdom, so that you may eat and drink at my table in my kingdom. . ." (Lk. 22:29-30; note also Lk. 23:42).

However, because people ate and drank with Jesus during his ministry does not assure them that they will eat and drink with him beyond history. To them Jesus will say,

> "Then you will begin to say, 'We ate and drank with you, and you taught in our streets.' But he will say, 'I do not know where you come from; go away from me, all you evildoers!' There will be weeping and gnashing of teeth when you see Abraham and Isaac and Jacob and all the prophets in the kingdom of God, and you yourselves thrown out. Then people will come from the east and west, from north and south, and will eat bread in the kingdom of God" (Lk. 13:26-29; note also the parables of the great banquet, Lk. 14:15-24, and of the pounds, Lk. 19:11-27).

What was the evil doing that excluded some? God's reign in Jesus reached out to include societal outcasts, persons whom "good religious folk" in his day excluded as "sinners." To exclude them was to "neglect justice and the love of God" (Lk. 11:42). Thus it is those who refuse to be inclusive who cannot be part of God's inclusive reign. I wanted my community to be inclusive in its outreach in our time.

Preaching and praying for God's reign

In my writings, I put much emphasis on preaching. Jesus proclaims and heralds God's reign (Lk., 4:43; 8:1; 9:11; Acts 1:3). He sends out the twelve and the seventy to proclaim it (Lk. 9:2; 10:9,11). Philip preaches God's reign (Acts 8:12) and so does Paul (Acts 19:8; 20:25; 28:23,31). These texts link preaching and God's reign directly together. However, the meaning is much the same as "witnessing," "preaching-good-news," and "speaking the word." All of them point to verbally proclaiming the message of what God has done to bring good news for all - the good news of mercy and forgiveness, liberty and justice, peace and joy for everyone in God's one human family.

Such a reign is something for which to pray. Jesus teaches his disciples to pray, "Your kingdom come" (Lk. 11:2). He assures his disciples with the words, "Do not be afraid, little flock, for your Father has-good-willed to give you the kingdom" (Lk. 12:32).[4]

I wanted for my community to enter into that same task of preaching and praying for God's reign in our time. We needed so much to experience that inclusive reign in our world.

Giving priority to God's reign

Jesus admonished his disciples, "do not worry about your life, what you will eat, or about your body, what you will wear" (Lk. 12:22). He assured them that God knows their needs. Then he said,

"Strive for God's kingdom, and these things will be given you as well"
(Lk. 12:31).

He then went on (in words quoted partly above),

"Do not be afraid, little flock, for your Father has-good-willed to give
you the kingdom. Sell your possessions, and give alms. Make pursues for
yourselves that do not wear out, an unfailing treasure in heaven, where
no thief comes near and no moth destroys. For where your treasure is,
there your heart will be also" (Lk. 12:32-34).

My community included both rich and poor, and I saw a deep need for us
to get our priorities straight. Material needs and possessions so easily could
become our prime concern. Then we would not put striving for God's reign first.
This is why I devote considerable space to the use of this world's goods. I tell
what Jesus said to one person.

"Take care! Be on your guard against all kinds of greed; for one's life
does not consist in the abundance of possessions" (Lk. 12:15; he goes on
to tell the parable of the rich fool, vss. 16-21).

On another occasion, he said,

"No slave can serve two masters; for a slave will either hate the one and
love the other, or be devoted to one and despise the other. You cannot
serve God and wealth" (Lk. 16:13).

There is the story of the callous rich man (Lk. 16:19-31) who would not
even help a poor man at his gate "who longed to satisfy his hunger with what fell
from the rich man's table; even the dogs would come and lick his sores" (vs. 21;
the rich man dies and ends up tormented in Hades).

There is the sad story of the admirable rich ruler whose possessions got in
the way of his following Jesus (Lk. 18:18-22). Jesus comments, "How hard it is
for those who have wealth to enter the kingdom of God!" Yet it is not impossible.
Jesus says, "What is impossible for mortals is possible for God" (Lk. 18:24).
Look what happened to the rich Zacchaeus (Lk. 19:1-10)!

In his "sermon on the plain," Jesus turns the usual human values upside down (note also Lk. 1:52).

> "Blessed are the poor, for yours is the kingdom of God" (Lk. 6:20).

> "But woe to you who are rich, for you have received your consolation" (Lk. 6:24).

In the world's eyes, it is the rich who are blessed and the poor who know woe. How can Jesus say what he does?

Is it because the priorities of the rich make for hands so graspingly full what there is no room for the blessing of God's reign? Is it that the poor have only empty hands to receive the blessed gift of letting God reign in their lives - of putting their trust in God, not in themselves or their possessions?

I wanted for my community and me really to give our priorities to God's reign, to "strive for God's kingdom" of compassion and mercy, of outreaching love to both friends and foe, of barrier-breaking justice and joy, across the boundaries of nation and language, gender and race, religion and social class.

My time had known enough of groups putting down one another. It was time again to experience God's lifting up all people and moving us toward being God's one joyous human family under God's gracious reign. It was a reign that could grow into a nesting tree and be like fermenting yeast to permeate our weary, hurting world (for these images see the parables of the kingdom, Lk. 13: 18-21).

What kind of a king

The background to "kingdom" language leads us back to the greatest of Israel's kings, David. The traditional understanding linked the expected Messiah to David's line and promised to restore Israel to heights of political power. The Infancy Stories link Jesus to such an expectation.

> "He will be great, and will be called Son of the Most High, and the Lord
> God will give to him the throne of his ancestor David. He will reign over
> the house of Jacob forever, and of his kingdom there will be no end"

(Lk. 1:32-33; similar references to David in Lk. 1:27,68-69; Acts 13:22-23).

Yet early Christians finally did not see Jesus simply as David's son and heir, another political-military leader, though even the first disciples did first see him in this way (note Lk. 24:21; Acts 1:6). Rather, we saw Jesus himself as calling David to witness that Jesus as Lord is not David's son.

> "Then he said to them, 'How can you say that the Messiah is David's son? For David himself says in the book of Psalms, "The Lord said to my Lord, 'Sit at my right hand, until I make your enemies your footstool'." David thus calls him Lord; so how can he be his son?'" (Lk. 20:41-42).

Jesus was not to be Israel's military-political Messiah-king. He also contrasted himself with other earthly kings.

> "A dispute arose among them as to which among them was to be regarded as the greatest. But he said them, 'The kings of the Gentiles lord it over them, and those in authority over them are called benefactors. But not so with you; rather the greatest among you must become like the youngest, and the leader one who serves. . . I am among you as one who serves" (22:24-27).

Jesus as servant stood in contrast to both Jewish and Gentile political-military leaders.[5]

> Toward the end of his life, Jesus entered Jerusalem to the cry,
>
> "Blessed is the king who comes in the name of the Lord!" (Lk. 19:38).

This may have expressed again the hope for a political-military leader. Religious leaders brought such charges against him to the Roman governor, Pilate.

> "They began to accuse him, saying, 'We found this man perverting our nation, forbidding us to pay taxes to the emperor, and saying that he himself is the Messiah, a king.' Then Pilate asked him, 'Are you king of the Jews?' He answered him, 'You say so.' Then Pilate said to the chief priests and the crowds, 'I find no basis for an accusation against him'" (Lk. 23:2-4; note also Acts 17:7).

He was not a political-military "king" to threaten the Romans. He was a servant king who saved others, but could not save himself. At his crucifixion,

> "the people stood by, watching; but the leaders scoffed at him, saying, 'He saved others; let him save himself if he is the Messiah of God, his chosen one!' The soldiers also mocked him, coming up and offering him sour wine, and saying, 'If you are the King of the Jews, save yourself!' There was an inscription over him, 'This is the King of the Jews'" (Lk. 23:35-38).

Even as he died, he "saved" others. He prayed for forgiveness for his crucifiers and promised a criminal paradise (23:34,43).

Jesus was the servant of a kingdom, God's kingdom, but it was not a kingdom of might but of mercy, not of crushing coercion but of compassionate caring, not of putting people down but of lifting people up to their dignity and worth as God's beloved children.

God's reign is a major theme in *Luke-Acts*. In our next conversation we turn to other major themes.

Endnotes

[1]Note for instance Ps. 96:10; 97:1; 99:1,4. Ps. 72:1-4 calls for earthly kings to reflect God's justice, righteousness, and concern for the poor and needy against the oppressor.

[2]See Lk. 17:22-23; 19:11; 21:7-9; Acts 1:7.

[3]There are four New Testament texts that tell of the Last Supper, each with distinct differences (I Cor. 11:23-26; Mk. 14:22-25; Mt. 26:26-29; Lk. 22:14-20). These differences point to a diversity among early Christians in the ways they celebrated the Lord's Supper.

[4]I think this translates the original Greek more accurately than "it is your Father's good pleasure to give you the kingdom" (NRSV).

[5]Roman emperors also could be called "benefactor," a term used in the quotation cited. It was Pilate, a representative of such benefactors, that finally acquiesced in Jesus' death, even while declaring him innocent three times.

CHAPTER 8
Other Major Themes

"My soul magnifies the Lord, and my spirit rejoices in God my Savior"
(Lk. 1:47).

The preceding chapters already have pointed to several key terms in my writings. In the verbal communication of the message I use "witness" (some 30 times), "proclaim-good-news" (some 25 times), "preach" (some 15 times), "teach" (some 30 times); and I refer to the Christian message as the "word" (some 40 times). Earlier chapters also have focused on titles for Jesus, the Holy Spirit, and the reign of God.

In this chapter I want to focus on five additional terms or family of terms. Two of them occur in the opening quotation, salvation (save, savior) and joy (rejoice). The others are repentance and forgiveness, prayer, and table.[1]

Save, salvation, savior

For me, this family of terms (I use them some 50 times) points to God's work in Jesus that brings wholeness and health to human life, both within history and beyond it. I use the noun "savior" four times, the noun "salvation" thirteen times, and the verb "save" some thirty times.

These terms do not have to do simply with personal salvation beyond death. They have to do with God's health-bringing purpose in all of life: physical health, psychic health, health in human relationships, health in the relationship with God, health in social and economic matters.

In the Infancy Stories Mary "rejoices in God my savior" (Lk. 1:47). The angels proclaim "a Savior who is the Messiah, the Lord." Zechariah sings of God's salvation (1:69,71,77); and old Simeon, having seen Jesus, says in his prayer, "my eyes have seen your salvation" (2:30). These uses of "savior" and "salvation" all point to God's health for the world in Jesus' coming. Both Peter and Paul can refer to Jesus as "savior" also (Acts 5:31; 13:23). These uses of "savior" all point to God's new health for the world in Jesus' coming.

The name "Jesus" (from the Hebrew, Joshua) itself means "God saves."[2] In stories of Jesus' healing, the term "save" clearly points to the health Jesus brings. "Daughter, your faith has made you well" (or "saved you," Lk. 8:48).[3] Peter and Paul also are instruments of God's healing (Acts 4:9; 14:9).

Yet God saves or heals more than the physical or psychic aspects of human life. God seeks health for the total self, the whole person. Entering into God's reign and losing oneself in God's healing purpose in Jesus "saves" the whole person. Jesus said, "For those who want to save their life will lose it, and those who lose their life for my sake will save it" (Lk. 9:24).[4] Jesus seeks and saves lost persons so they may know a new relationship with God in every aspect of their life (Lk. 19:10).

But the one who saved others did not seek to save himself (Lk. 23:35,39). He was willing even to die to be faithful to God. Yet his death was not the end. In his resurrection, early Christians came to see and proclaim their crucified and risen Lord as God's saving, health-bringing deed for both Jews (Acts 2:47; 13:26) and Gentiles (Acts 13:47; 28:28). As Isaiah proclaimed, "all flesh shall see the salvation of God" (quoted in Lk. 3:6).

I want to point to two additional texts where I use the word "salvation," one in *Luke* and one in *Acts*. In the story about Zacchaeus (Lk. 19:1-10), Jesus reaches out to this despised tax collector. Why was he despised? Because he collaborated with Rome to collect taxes and exploited his own people by adding to the tax to enrich himself.

His name, Zacchaeus, means "righteous," but his actions contradicted the meaning of his own name. Jesus gave him the chance to change and really live out his name.

Jesus calls his name and enters into a personal relationship with Zacchaeus. He defies custom by going to be in the home of this despised "sinner." Jesus' contact transformed Zacchaeus. It brought 1) a personal relationship with Jesus, 2) a new presence in his home and family, 3) a change in his work: restitution for wrong and no more fraud, 4) a new public concern in caring for the poor: he gave away half his wealth.

After all this, then Jesus says, "Today salvation has come to this house" (Lk. 19:9). Salvation meant that Zacchaeus' whole self had been transformed: his life, his home, his work, his sense of public responsibility. Now as a descendant of Abraham and God's promise to be a blessing (Gen. 12:3; 22:18), his life turned from being a blight to being a blessing.

The use of "salvation" in a text in *Acts* follows Peter's healing of a lame man "in the name of Jesus Christ of Nazareth" (Acts 3:1-10). To those who reject Jesus, Peter later then says, "There is salvation in no one else; for there is no other name under heaven given among mortals by which we must be saved" (Acts 4:12).

Does this mean that only Jesus himself "saves"? What does "name" mean? In the Hebrew heritage, the name of someone expresses that person's essence and purpose. The name "Jesus" means "*God* saves." The title "Christ" means "*God's* anointed." So, to speak of the *name* of Jesus Christ is to focus on *God* at work in him. There is no salvation apart from such a saving God. This living, saving God of all creation is at work in Jesus, a particular person in human history, but not only in him.

Jesus himself, in his hometown synagogue, points to God at work in Elijah to feed the widow of Zarepath in Sidon; in Elisha to heal the Syrian leper Naaman (Lk. 4:25-27). He would not let his own people limit God's saving work.

Jesus would not let his disciples stop someone who cast out demons in Jesus' name ("God saves") but did not follow them. He said to them, "Do not stop him; for whoever is not against you is for you" (Lk. 9:49-50). We cannot limit the God at work in Jesus to followers of Jesus. The way God is at work in Jesus may also be the way God is at work elsewhere. The "name of Jesus Christ" points to the God who is at work to save and heal and bring health everywhere to all of God's beloved children.

I wanted my community to be instruments of that salvation, that health, in our time. I wanted them to look for where God was at work in others beyond our community and to join forces with them. Our commitment to Jesus did not limit us. It was precisely our commitment to his name that opened us to the God who works to bring health through many different people in many different places of our world.

Joy, rejoice

What is one major result of God's health-bringing work? I place an emphasis on joy. I use "joy" (*chara*) and "rejoice" (*charein*) language more than twenty times. In its Greek form, joy (*chara*) is linked closely to grace (*charis*). We might say that joy has its roots in God's grace, God's favor, toward us and all the world. As the early missionary Barnabas came to Antioch, "when he saw the *grace* of God, he *rejoiced*" (Acts 11:23).[5]

In the Infancy Stories, the expectation of John the Baptist's birth brings joy, gladness, and rejoicing (Lk. 1:14). Jesus' birth is "good news of great joy for all the people" (Lk. 2:10). At the presence of Jesus in Mary's womb, John leaps for joy in Elizabeth's womb (Lk. 1:44), and Mary "rejoices in God my Savior" (Lk. 1:47).[6]

In his ministry, Jesus himself rejoices in the Holy Spirit and gives thanks to God (Lk. 10:21). The seventy whom Jesus sent out rejoice over their success, but Jesus tells them rather to "rejoice that your names are written in heaven" (Lk. 10:17-20).

There is joy when a sinner repents (Lk. 15:7,10) and when a brother "was dead, and has come to life...was lost, and is found" (Lk. 15:32). A despised tax collector rejoices when Jesus goes home with him (Lk. 19:6). Jesus' entry into Jerusalem brings rejoicing over God's mighty deeds" (Lk. 19:37), and the presence of the risen Lord brings joy (Lk. 24:41,52).

I tell also of much rejoicing in *Acts*, even in the midst of persecution: "they rejoiced that they were considered worthy to suffer dishonor for the sake of the name of Jesus" (Acts 5:41). The healing of people brings joy (Acts 8:7-8). The Ethiopian eunuch rejoices over his baptism and understanding of the good news (Acts 8:39). Barnabas (as noted earlier) rejoices over God's grace in the church at Antioch, and Rhoda has joy over Peter's release from prison (Acts 12:14).

Gentiles rejoice over their inclusion in God's salvation (Acts 13:47-48), and that joy occurs in various geographical areas. At Iconium "the disciples were filled with joy and the Holy Spirit (Acts 13:51). In Phoenicia and Samaria the conversion of the Gentiles "brought great joy to all the believers" (Acts 15:3). In Antioch the congregation rejoices over a letter from the Jerusalem church (Acts 15:30-31).

The earliest Christians "ate their food with joyous hearts (Acts 2:46), and the Philippian jailer "and his entire household rejoiced that he had become a believer in God" (Acts 16:34).[7]

Joy occurs in many different contexts. What ties them together is what God graciously has done in Jesus Christ to bring "good news of great joy for all the people." I wanted my community and people throughout the Empire to know that joy - that deep sense of relationship with God in all of life's circumstances.

Repentance and forgiveness

What response to God's gift of good news can lead to joy? That gift calls for repentance (*metanoia*, "mind change") and forgiveness (*aphesis*, "letting go"). Repentance is not simply saying, "I'm sorry." It involves the "mind-change" of a new direction. Forgiveness is not saying, "I'll forgive, but I'll never forget." It is to "let go" of the past in taking a new direction. In a text from the prophet Jeremiah, God speaks to Israel and "lets go." "I will forgive their iniquity, and remember their sin no more" (Jer. 31:34).

I link repentance and forgiveness together several times. My writings also use them separately,[8] but here I want to deal with texts where they occur together.

The terms did not begin with Jesus' ministry. They are part of Israel's history. John the Baptist, as preparer of Jesus' way, also proclaimed "a baptism of repentance for the forgiveness of sins" (Lk. 3:3; note also Acts 13:24; 19:4).

For me, they now become a decisive part of the Christian missionary message. After his ministry, death, and resurrection, Jesus commissioned his disciples, "that repentance and forgiveness of sins is to be proclaimed in his name to all nations, beginning from Jerusalem" (Lk. 24:47). But here it is important to note that the proclamation of good news in Jesus precedes and provides the basis for repentance and forgiveness of sins.

What do I mean by "sins"? I mean whatever destroys and fails to build relationships with God or with other people. A sin is not simply this or that bad deed. Such misdeeds result from the deeper sins of breaking relationships; and the breaking of relationship with God leads to the breakdown between and among persons. Repentance means basically to turn from such destructive, sinful behavior - to change one's mind from destroying to building, from breaking relationships to establishing them.

God's good news in Jesus is God's act of reaching out to build a new relationship with us. Our response is to repent, to turn to that outreaching gift and let go of our destructive sins, for God already has built a way to us in the good news.

In his Pentecost sermon, Peter ties together repentance, baptism, forgiveness, and the Holy Spirit.

> "Repent, and be baptized everyone of you in the name of Jesus Christ so that your sins may be forgiven, and you will receive the Holy Spirit" (Acts 2:38; see also 3:19).

To turn and enter in baptism into all that Jesus stands for is to let go of the past and be empowered by the Spirit to lead a new life of building relationships in every aspect of human life. This message of repentance and forgiveness is for both Jews (Acts 5:31; 8:22) and Gentiles (Acts 11:18; 20:21; 26:20).

I wanted my community to understand more fully how God's good news in Jesus does enable us to change our minds, to let go of the distortions of our lives (God has "let go"!), and to enter into God's gift of new life and joy.

Pray, prayer[9]

To receive and enter into God's gift is not simply a one-time matter. It calls for constant nurturing and renewal. For me this includes a life of prayer, a strong emphasis in my writings. One can see this by comparing my *Luke* with similar settings in Mark's Gospel. Where Mark says nothing about Jesus praying, I relate an event to Jesus praying (examples below). Throughout his ministry, Jesus communicated with God repeatedly to open himself again and again to God's renewing power for his mission. For my community and me, I wanted to show that a life of prayer is rooted in the example of Jesus.

In my writings I point to various kinds of prayer: prayers of praise, prayers of thanksgiving, prayers of petition for the one(s) who prays, prayers of intercession for others.[10] On the one hand, prayer is responding and speaking *to* God; on the other hand, it is an openness and listening to receive *from* God God's sustaining gifts for life and renewing power for God's mission. Let me point to various places where prayer occurs in *Luke-Acts*.

In the Infancy Stories, John the Baptist's father Zechariah prays for a son (Lk. 1:10-13) and blesses God (1:68). Mary magnifies the Lord (1:46). The devout

Simeon praises God and prays for a peaceful dismissal (2:28-29). The prophetess Anna prays and praises God for God's redeeming deed (2:37-38).

I wanted to emphasize that Jesus was born into a context of praying people. As I tell the story, from the very beginning, Jesus was part of a worshiping community (see 2:22-24,39-52).

I put more emphasis than Mark on Jesus' praying at crucial moments. He prays at his baptism, with God's announcement of his identity and his empowerment by the Spirit for his mission (Lk.3:21). He retreats to the wilderness for a time of renewing prayer when the multitudes put pressure on him (5:16; Mk 1:35). He spends a night in prayer before choosing his disciples (6:12). He asks the crucial question of his identity in the context of prayer (9:18-20). He prays when he is transfigured and God reaffirms his identity (9:28-36).

One text presents his agonizing prayer as he faces death.

> "Father, if you are willing, remove this cup from me; yet not my will but yours be done...In his anguish he prayed more earnestly, and his sweat became like great drops of blood falling down on the ground" (Lk. 22:42-44).

And as he dies, he prays, "Father, into your hands I commend my spirit" (Lk. 23:46, from Ps. 31:5). All of these point to Jesus' prayer life as renewing empowerment for his mission and for facing death.

When he fed the multitudes, he looked to heaven, blessed the loaves and fish (Lk. 9:16). He gave thanks at the Last Supper with his disciples (22:17,19). He thanked God for revealing to infants what is hidden from the wise (10:21).

He also prayed for others. He prayed that Simon Peter's faith would not fail (Lk. 22:31). He even prayed for forgiveness for those who crucified him (Lk. 23:34). Here he did what he taught: "pray for those who abuse you" (Lk. 6:28).

He encouraged and taught his disciples to pray. Here we think first of what came to be called the Lord's Prayer (11:1-4),[11] with both its opening prayer of adoration and its several petitions. He told a story that pointed them to being persistent in prayer (Lk. 11:5-10; see also 18:1-8) and to God's willingness to give them the Holy Spirit for the asking (11:11-13). He also taught them to pray for strength when times were tough (21:36) and when they, like he, faced temptation (22:40,45-46).

In the parable of the Pharisee and tax collector (18:9-14) he contrasted the self-righteousness "prayer" of the one with the humble prayer of the other:

"God, I thank you that I am not like other people . . . even like this tax collector . . . (18:11).

"God, be merciful to me, a sinner" (18:13).

Jesus taught that the second "justifies" - that is, opens one to a relationship with God that God lifts up. True prayer never can be a matter of self-exaltation but of open reliance on God's mercy and God's power to lift the lowly (see also Lk. 1:52).

In *Acts* I tell how important prayer was also for the earliest followers of Jesus after his resurrection. They wait in prayer for their empowering by the Spirit (Acts 1:14). They pray in choosing one to replace Judas, Jesus' betrayer, in order to make the number of twelve disciples complete again (1:24).

Prayer is an essential part of their nurture for their mission (2:42; 4:31; 6:4) and they continue to pray in the temple (3:1; 22:17; note also Lk. 24:53). They pray to receive the Holy Spirit (8:15; note Lk. 11:13), and the encounter between Saul and Ananias involves prayer (9:10-12). Prayer empowers Peter to restore Tabitha to life (9:40) and Paul to heal Publius (28:8).

God hears Cornelius' prayers (10:2-4,30-31), and the revelation to Peter to include Gentiles occurs in prayer (10:9; 11:15). The church prays for Peter when he is in prison (12:5,12), and the prayers of Paul and Silas lead to an earthquake that shakes the prison's foundations (16:25-26; note also 16:13,16).

From these many examples, I wanted my community to see that both Jesus and the earliest Christians were people of prayer. We needed to follow their example as people of prayer in our mission as well.

The table

Finally, the table theme was very important to me. Who eats with whom was a crucial issue in Jesus' time. Some religious folk would not eat with persons who did not fit into their religious system nor conform to their rules (I touched on this earlier). These persons who could not or would not conform were religious and social outcasts. Jesus broke through such excluding attitudes and wanted to see everyone at the table of God's human family.

I tell the story of a dinner party where Jesus was at table in the home of one Pharisee (Lk. 7:36-50). A sinful woman of the city (probably a prostitute) crashed that party, bringing an alabaster jar of ointment. She wept, bathed Jesus' feet with her tears, dried them with her hair, kissed and anointed his feet.

It incensed the Pharisee that Jesus let such a woman to the table. Jesus responded by lifting up the great love she showed, forgiving her sins, praising her healing faith, and sending her out in peace, in *shalom*, in wholeness of life. Jesus wanted to include people at a table of love and forgiveness, healing and peace.

What we might call table fellowship occurred also in the story of Jesus' feeding the five thousand (Lk. 9:10-17). His disciples wanted to send the crowd away to fend for themselves, but Jesus said to them, "You give them something to eat." Many in that crowd would not have been welcome in some "religious" homes, but Jesus made them welcome at his table and satisfied their hunger.

At another dinner party, this time on a sabbath (Lk. 14:1-24) Jesus healed a man with dropsy (edema). He challenged the rule that forbid healing on the sabbath. For Jesus, to meet a human need was more important than keeping a rule, especially when the sabbath itself was to be a day of renewal and restoration.

At the same dinner party, Jesus challenged those who sought honored places at the table.

> "For all who exalt themselves will be humbled, and those who humble themselves will be exalted" (vs. 11).

He challenged further those who invite people to their tables.

"When you give a luncheon or dinner, do not invite your friends or your brothers or your relatives or rich neighbors, in case they may invite you in return, and you would be repaid. But when you give a banquet, invite the poor, the crippled, the lame, and the blind. And you will be blessed, because they cannot repay you, for you will be paid at the resurrection of the just" (vss. 12-14; see also vs. 21).

"Good" society often rejected persons with disabilities, sometimes charging that their sin caused their condition.[12] But Jesus reached out to include such persons and make them welcome.

I want to point to two final tables scenes in *Luke*, one before and one after Jesus' death and resurrection. The first is the Last Supper (Lk. 22:14-23). There Jesus fed the disciples with himself: "This is myself" ("self" is a better translation of the Greek *soma* than "body"). He gave them himself, his life and ministry, his death and resurrection, to be in and live through them.

In the words, "This cup that is poured out for you is the new covenant in my blood,"[13] Jesus poured God's love into them to let that love build community. Covenant language points to community-building, and blood language points to life poured out in love for others.

I wanted my community to understand, when we eat the bread, we receive all for which Jesus stands into ourselves to live in us. When we drink the cup, we pour God's love in him into ourselves to let it flow in us to build community - right there among us at the table and then out to all those other tables of our world that need so much to know God's flowing love.

The other table scene is the risen Jesus with two disciples at Emmaus (Lk. 24:28-35). There at table, as Jesus "took bread, blessed and broke it, and gave it to them," they finally recognized who he was (vss. 30-31). And from the vantage point of the table - his giving himself to them there, they could look back and know that he was with them, even when they did not recognize him (vs. 32). But then he vanished from them. They could not capture his presence there. They had no monopoly on him. They set out to tell the story, but the other disciples too had known and would know his risen presence (vss. 33-36).

I wanted my community to know that the risen Jesus still broke bread with us in our worship. That worship gave us a vantage point to look back for his presence on the road of our lives, as well as to look forward to telling our story and sharing the story of others, how they had known his risen presence too.

I tell also in *Acts* how the "breaking of the bread" continued among early Christians after Pentecost. It was part of their nourishment for their mission.

> "They devoted themselves to the apostles' teaching and fellowship, to the breaking of bread, and the prayers" (Acts 2:42; note also vs. 46 and Acts 20:7).

Further, Peter's vision (Acts 10:9-16) overcame the divisive conflict between Jews and Gentiles over eating at the same table. Peter proclaimed, "I truly understand that God shows no partiality, but in every nation anyone who fears him and does what is right is acceptable to him" (Acts 10:34).

God wants no table that excludes anyone. God wants a table that includes all kinds of people in one saved, joyous, repentant, forgiven, prayerful human family. That's what I wanted for my church community too.

How do I understand the life of that community? To this we turn in our next conversation.

Endnotes

[1]The major themes in this chapter occur more frequently than in any other of the gospels.

[2]Matthew's Gospel makes this very explicit: "you are to name him *Jesus*, for he will *save* his people from their sins (Mt. 1:21.

[3]Similar texts include Lk. 7:50; 8:36,50; 17:19; 18:42; Acts 4:9; 14:9.

[4]To save one's life is not an end in itself. It becomes the byproduct of investing oneself in God's purpose as expressed in Jesus.

[5]Joy is not the same as happiness. The latter comes from the root "hap," meaning luck or good fortune. Happiness can be here today and gone tomorrow. Not so joy that is rooted in God's amazing grace.

[6]In these last two instances Luke uses another Greek word for rejoice, *agalliasthai.*

[7]These instances also use the same Greek word family as in the previous endnote.

[8]Luke uses "forgiveness" language in Lk. 1:77; 5:20; 7:47; 11:4; 12:10; 23:34; Acts 10:43; 13:38; 26:18; "repentance" language in Lk.5:32; 15:7,10; Acts 20:21; 26:20. Lk. 17:3 and Acts 8:22 link the two.

[9]The primary Greek words for pray and prayer are *proseuchesthai* and *proseuche.* Less common are *deisthai* and *deesis.*

[10]To my knowledge, Luke includes no *prayers* of confession. Perhaps his use of "repentance" language takes their place.

[11]This is Luke's version. The one with which we are more familiar is Matthew's (Mt. 6:9-13).

[12]We can see this clearly expressed in John 9:2.

CHAPTER 9

My Understanding of the Church

"Meanwhile the church through Judea, Galilee, Samaria had peace and was built up. Living in the fear (awe) of the Lord and in the comfort (advocacy, support) of the Holy Spirit, it increased in numbers" (Acts 9:31).

I first use the word "church" (*ekklesia*, sometimes translated "congregation" or "assembly")[1] in *Acts*, there some 20 times.[2] For me it is the community of those, "called out" into Jesus' mission *after* his resurrection, his commission of the apostles, and their empowerment by the Holy Spirit. The church is people (not a building), the community of the risen Christ, empowered to share a message of God's good news "to the ends of the earth."

Solidarity with Israel

The church community has deep, historical roots in Israel. Israel's *twelve* patriarchs ("leading fathers") and Jesus' *twelve* apostles are linked as God's covenant communities.[3] God's covenant with and promise to Abraham are central (I refer to Abraham some 20 times). After Pentecost, Peter proclaims to his Jewish hearers,

"You are the descendants of the prophets and the covenant God gave to your ancestors, saying to Abraham, 'And in your descendants all the families of the earth shall be blessed'" (Acts 3:25; note also Lk. 1:55,73; Acts 13:26).

The universal mission of Jesus' disciples has its roots in the universal ("all the families of the earth") promise to Abraham. I tell also how Paul applies Isaiah's portrayal of God's call to Israel to his hearers' Gentile mission.

> "I have set you to be a light for the Gentiles, so that you may bring salvation to the ends of the earth" (Acts 13:47, quoting Is. 49:6).

Israel's past mission has become the church's present mission.

But there also is a link to Israel in the future. I tell how Jesus speaks of a time

> "when you (will) see Abraham and Isaac and Jacob and all the prophets in the kingdom of God . . . Then people will come from the east and west, from north and south, and will eat in the kingdom of God" (Lk. 13:28-29; see also Lk. 16:19-31; 20:37-38; 22:28-30).

The church has this solidarity with Israel in terms both of the past and the future. Those roots nurture and help give life and direction to God's universal mission and blessing for "all the families of the earth."

The Infancy Stories (Lk. 1-2) show strong ties to Israel. Elizabeth and Zechariah, Mary and Joseph, Simeon and Anna, John the Baptist and Jesus, all are part of that community, fully observant of its customs, and rooted in its scriptures. The missions of both John and Jesus tie into Israel.

John will "turn many of the people of Israel to the Lord their God . . . to make ready a people prepared for the Lord" (Lk. 1:16-17; note also Lk. 1:76-77). Jesus will "reign over the house of Jacob forever" (Lk. 1:33). Mary sings that God "has helped his servant Israel (Lk. 1:54). Zechariah proclaims, "Blessed be the Lord God of Israel, for he has looked favorably upon his people and redeemed them" (Lk. 1:68). Simeon refers to Jesus as "a light for revelation to the Gentiles and for glory to your people Israel" (Lk. 2:32).

The Infancy Stories point both backward to this tie with Israel in the past and forward to Jesus' ministry in the rest of *Luke*. Jesus and the community of his disciples are linked inseparably to their roots in Israel and its scriptures.[4]

The disciples of Jesus

Though I only speak of the "church' *after* Jesus' resurrection, here I want to write about the community of Jesus' disciples *before* it. Early in his ministry, Jesus begins to call others to follow him in his mission. The first are Peter, James, and John. In the story of the amazing catch of fish (Lk. 5:1-11), Jesus turns it into a call to mission.

> "Do not be afraid; from now on you will be catching people. When they had brought their boats ashore, they left everything and followed him" (vss. 10-11).

So did the tax collector Levi (Lk. 5:27-28).

Jesus' disciples ("students of a teacher") journey with him earlier (Lk. 6:1), but soon he chose twelve of them, naming them apostles ("those sent with a mission"). For me, only the twelve bear that title (Lk. 6:12-16). As the twelve patriarchs were the core of Israel's covenant community, so the twelve *apostles* were the core of the new covenant community.

However, the circle around Jesus was not limited to the twelve. As he went through cities and villages preaching and bringing good news, "the twelve were with him, as well as some women. . . Mary, called Magdalene. . . Joanna. . . Suzanna, and many others, who provided for them our of their resources" (Lk. 8:1-3; note also Lk. 23:49,55).

At a time when many often limited the role of women to the care of home and family, I wanted to emphasize their partnership with men in Jesus' ministry (I use the word "woman" nearly 40 times in *Luke* and 20 times in *Acts*). It is women who first tell of Jesus' resurrection, while the male apostles first regarded this an "an idle tale" (Lk. 24:10,22-24). Society then, even Jesus' own disciples, also shunted children aside, but Jesus welcomed them (Lk. 18:15-16).

As his students, the mission of Jesus' disciples was to resemble his.

"Then Jesus called the twelve together and gave them power and
authority over all demons and to cure diseases, and he sent them to
proclaim the kingdom of God and to heal" (Lk. 9:1-2).

I tell also how Jesus expanded the mission of the twelve by sending out seventy
more.

"The harvest is plentiful, but the laborers are few; therefore ask the Lord
of the harvest to send out laborers into his harvest" (Lk. 10:2).

They too are to "cure the sick...and say...'The kingdom of God has come near to
you" (Lk. 10:9); and they can expect both acceptance and rejection (Lk. 10:3-11;
note also 9:4-5).

Jesus instructed his disciples what it means to follow the Messiah, Son of
Man, in his suffering, rejection, and death:

"If any want to become my followers, let them deny themselves and take
up their cross daily and follow me. For those who want to save their life
will lose it, and those who lose their life for my sake will save it'" (Lk.
9:23-24; see also Lk. 14:15-24,25-33).

When his disciples dispute about greatness, Jesus pointed them to being servants
(Lk. 22:24--27).

Jesus called his followers to bear fruit. This taps into the "vineyard" as
a symbol for Israel's fruit-bearing (Is. 5:1-7; see Lk. 13:6-9; 20:9-16). In the
"Sermon on the Plain," Jesus points to some of that fruit: loving enemies, doing
good to those who hate you, blessing those who curse you, praying for those who
abuse you, being merciful as God is merciful, not judging nor condemning (Lk.
6:27-38; note also vs. 43).

As we saw in the previous chapter, Jesus also wanted his disciples to be
a community of prayer. He had to challenge the misuse of the temple. As the
center of Israel's life, it was to be a prayerful place of healing and wholeness.
That is why Jesus

> "entered the temple and began to drive out those who were selling things there; and he said, 'It is written, "My house shall be a house of prayer"; but you have made it a den of robbers" (Lk. 19:45-46).

The temple belonged to Jesus' disciples too (Lk. 24:53).

Like Jesus' disciples, I wanted my community to follow Jesus daily: proclaiming God's reign, healing human illness, showing Jesus' self-giving love, serving, bearing fruit, praying. I wanted them, like Jesus, to challenge systems and rules that did not serve to build up and include all kinds of persons in a welcoming and compassionate community.

The community in Acts

For me, the church is both the local and larger community of the risen Messiah, commissioned by him and empowered by the Holy Spirit. I do not limit my references to that community to the word "church" (*ekklesia*). In fact, I use it for the first time in chapter 5 (Acts 5:11). However, here let me point to some places where I do use "church."

As the opening quotation from *Acts* in this chapter indicates, the church is a growing body of persons across the Empire who believe in the good news (Acts 9:31; also 16:5). In fact, *Acts* as a whole is the story of building up that community, though many texts tell of that upbuilding without using the word church.[5]

What are other places where I do use it? The Jerusalem church knew persecution with Saul "ravaging the church" (Acts 8:1-3). King Herod "laid violent hands upon some who belonged to the church" (Acts 12:1). After being stoned and dragged out of Lystra, Paul and Barnabas, acknowledging many persecutions in entering God's reign, strengthened and encouraged others and "appointed elders in every church" (Acts 14:22-23). Returning to Antioch, they "called the church together and related all God had done with them, and how he had opened a door of faith for the Gentiles" (Acts 14:27).

I refer to the local church in several locations: in Jerusalem (Acts 11:22), in Antioch (11:26), in Caesarea (18:22). Traffic and conversation occur between the churches in Antioch and Jerusalem to settle a dispute (Acts 15:1-35). At Miletus, Paul said to the elders of the church at Ephesus:

> "Keep watch over yourselves and over the flock, of which the Holy
> Spirit has made you overseers, to shepherd the church of God" (Acts
> 20:28).

My use of the plural "elders" (*presbuteroi*)[6] points to a shared approach in the leadership of local churches.

I refer to the community of Christians in several other ways. The following points to two of them, "disciples" and "the Way."

> "Meanwhile Saul, still breathing threats and murder against the *disciples*
> of the Lord, went to the high priest and asked for letters to the synagogue
> in Damascus, so that if he found any who belonged to *the Way*, men nor
> women, he might bring them bound to Jerusalem" (Acts 9:1-2).

The "disciples of the Lord" are not the twelve apostles but ordinary followers of Jesus. I use the word "disciples" many times to refer to the community of Christians.[7] I also refer to "the Way" several times.[8] As to the word "Christian" itself, I use it twice: "it was in Antioch that the disciples were first called Christians (Acts 11:26; see also 26:28).

I want to refer to the community of Christians in one more way: "believers" or "those who believed" (in Jesus as the Messiah). "To believe" is not simply an intellectual affirmation *about* Jesus. It is entering with one's whole self into the good news in him and letting it direct every aspect of life. It is a word for both Jews (Acts 4:1-4) and Gentiles (Acts 13:48; 15:7).[9]

One text expresses very directly a concern for believing in Jesus. In the story of the Philippian jailer (part of Acts 16:16-40), the jailer asks, "Sirs, what must I do to be saved?" Paul and Silas answer, "Believe on the Lord Jesus, and you will be saved, you and your household" (Acts 16:30-31).

However, in the story, believing in Jesus does not end there. Rather, ''he and his entire household rejoiced that he had become a believer *in God*'' (vs. 34). To believe in the Lord Jesus is to believe in the "Lord God of Israel" (Lk. 1:68).

So for me there is no single way to refer to the community of faith in *Acts*. Christians are the church, disciples of the Lord, people of the Way, believers in Jesus. Early Christians used a diversity of names. Yet there were some distinguishing marks among them.

Marks of the community in Acts

1. Witness[10]

The whole story of *Acts* is the unfolding of Jesus' commission to the twelve apostles.

> "But you shall receive power when the Holy Spirit has come upon you;
> and you shall be my witnesses . . . to the end of the earth" (Acts 1:8).

Though the twelve apostles are the foundational witnesses - those who had known Jesus in both his ministry and his resurrection, they were not the only ones. Waiting with them in prayer before Pentecost were also "certain women, including Mary the mother of Jesus, as well as his brothers" (Acts 1:14). Further, Peter applies Joel's prophecy to Christians. God declares "that I will pour out my Spirit upon all flesh, and your sons and daughters shall prophesy ("speak for" God, Acts 2:17).

Witnesses throughout *Acts* include a number of persons who were not apostles: Barnabas, Symeon, Lucius, Manaen, Saul/Paul (Acts 13:1); Mark, Silas, Timothy (Acts 15:39-40); Apollos (18:24); Timothy and Erastus (19:22); Sopater, Aristarchus, Secundus, Gaius, Tychicus, Trophimus (20:4). There also was Cornelius (Acts 10); Lydia (16:14,40); a slave girl (16:16-18); Aquila and Priscilla (18:2,26). The task of witnessing needs many voices.

For me this had to include a special concern for women. With the strong patriarchal mentality in both Israel and the church, I wanted to see more balance by lifting up Mary, God's daughters (from Joel), Lydia, a slave girl, Priscilla, as well as many unnamed women.

> "Yet more than ever believers were added to the Lord, great numbers of both men and women" (Acts 5:14; see also Acts 8:3,12; 22:4).

> "Many of them therefore believed, including not a few Greek women and men of high standing" (Acts 17:12).

I wanted my community to see the earliest Christians as a witnessing community of both women and men. I wanted the still widely prevailing gender barrier to go down for the sake of mutuality in mission together.

2. Learning and worship

Jesus himself stood firmly in the learning and worship tradition of Israel and the synagogue. He interpreted his mission in his hometown synagogue (Lk. 4:14-21) and taught in other synagogues (Lk. 4:15,31-33,44; 6:6; 13:10).

That relationship to the synagogue continued among early Christians as I tell the story in *Acts*. As their witness spread across the Empire, Paul, for instance, often went there first.

> "For several days he was with the disciples in Damascus, and immediately he began to proclaim Jesus in the synagogues, saying, 'He is the Son of God'" (Acts 9:19-20).

He proclaimed the message in the synagogues of Cyprus (13:5), in Antioch in Pisidia (13:14-47), in Iconium (14:1), in Thessalonica (17:1-3), in Beroea (17:10-11), in Athens (17:16-17), in Corinth (18:4), in Ephesus (18:19; 19:8).

With all the first Christians as Jews, the synagogue's worship and prayer, teaching and scripture interpretation, gave them their pattern.

One text puts these elements together in the experience of the earliest Christians.

> "They devoted themselves to the apostles' teaching and fellowship, to the breaking of bread and the prayers" (Acts 2:42).

Teaching, fellowship (*koinonia*, partnership), the Lord's Supper ("breaking of bread"), and prayer were essential to nurturing the internal life of the community. The early Christians also shared in supporting one another economically (Acts 2:44-45; 4:32-35; 6:1-3).

Without entirely separating teaching and preaching,[11] teaching[12] is more for those who already have entered into the community. Preaching[13] is more for those outside it who have yet to hear the message.

To nurture and support one another within the community - in teaching, breaking bread, praying, and providing for material needs, enables the community then to preach and bear witness to those outside the community in the wider society.

I wanted for my community to be such a nurturing and learning community, in order that we too might let God's Holy Spirit empower us for the mission in our time.

3. Healing

As I tell the story in *Acts*, the ministry of early Christians followed Jesus, not only in his preaching and teaching but in his healing.

In the name of Jesus, Peter and John heal a man lame from birth (Acts 3:1-10), setting off reverberations (Acts 3:11-16; 4:5-12). Many sick people from towns around Jerusalem are cured (5:16). The apostles do "signs and wonders" (4:43), and the "signs and great miracles" performed by Philip amaze Simon the magician (8:13). Peter heals the bedridden and paralyzed Aeneas (9:34-35) and restores Tabitha to life (9:36-42).

Paul heals a man crippled from birth (14:10) and frees a slave girl from an enslaving spirit (16:16-18). "God did extraordinary miracles through Paul" (19:11). A young man, Eutychus, who fell asleep while Paul was preaching and fell three stories from a window, some thought dead, but Paul reassured them, "Do not be alarmed, for his life is in him (20:10). On his voyage to Rome, he cured the island chief Publius' father of fever and dysentery and others of their diseases (28:7-9).

I wanted these examples of healing among the earliest Christians to show that Jesus' healing ministry continued through them. Nor did it stop with them. Now that healing ministry could continue through my community as well.

4. Confrontation

The mission of the first Christians included not only a witness of preaching, teaching, healing, and nurturing the community. It included also confronting religious and political power and taking public action.

Peter and John's healing of a man in the name of Jesus caused religious authorities to charge them not to speak or teach anymore in Jesus' name. But Peter and John responded,

> "Whether it is right in God's sight to listen to you rather than God, you
> must judge; for we cannot keep from speaking about what we have seen
> and heard" (Acts 4:20).

Later, authorities arrested them but God's angel ("messenger") freed them. Again authorities charged them.

> "'We gave you strict orders not to teach in this name, yet you have filled
> Jerusalem with your teaching . . .' But Peter and the apostles answered,
> 'We must obey God rather than any human authority . . .'" (5:28-29).

The highest religious authority could not silence those empowered by God's Spirit to teach and proclaim the good news of Jesus as the Messiah. One respected Pharisee, Gamaliel, said to the authorities:

> "I tell you, keep away from these men and let them alone; because if this
> plan or this undertaking is of human origin, it will fail; but if it is of
> God, you will not be able to overthrow them - in that case you may even
> be found fighting against God!" (5:38-39).

Stephen also confronted religious authorities. He was stoned to death with Saul/Paul's approval (7:51-8:1). This was before Paul's big turnaround. After it, on his mission, Paul himself suffered death threats and plots to kill him (9:23-25,28-30; 20:3,18-24).

King Herod handled some people from the Jerusalem church violently, killed the apostle James, and arrested Peter (12:1-3), though through prayer again God's messenger freed him (vs. 7; read 12:1-23 for the whole story).

Paul faced further challenges (see 13:44-47; 14:1-7). In Lystra he was stoned and dragged from the city as dead, but with supportive disciples he recovered (14:19-20). His freeing a slave girl from her personal and economic bondage, thereby depriving her exploitive owners of monetary gain, led to the collaboration of economic, political, and police powers against Paul and Silas. They were beaten publicly and thrown in jail. (Acts 16:16-40 tells the whole story.)

After their singing and praying, an earthquake thundered against such penal injustice and opened the prison, but they did not run. Rather, they seized the opportunity to lead the jailer and his household into faith in Jesus.[14]

Further, after public officials learned that Paul was a Roman citizen and wanted to let Paul and Silas go secretly, Paul would not let them escape public accountability for what they had done. God's witnesses speak against personal and public injustice. I do need to say that sometimes, when Paul experienced religious attacks, political authorities saved him.[15]

Finally Paul knew that struggle awaited him in Jerusalem, but he was "ready not only to be bound but even to die in Jerusalem for the name of the Lord Jesus" (21:10-14).

I did not want my community to think that Christian witness was without struggle and suffering, even death (it meant that for Jesus, Stephen, James, Peter, Paul). Yet I wanted to create a climate where no one needs to feel threatened anymore nor needs to attack and kill others. After all, the message is one of good news of great joy for all the people.

In the midst of the world's life, the church, rooted in Israel and in the promise to Abraham to be a blessing, is called to be a community of witness, of worship and learning, of healing, and yes - where it still must be - of confronting those powers who defy justice and joy and peace. It is to be a community ready, like Paul, even to die for the name of the Lord Jesus.

With this understanding of the church, how might what I wanted for the world in my time intersect with what you want for yours? I will discuss this in our last conservation.

Endnotes

[1]See Acts 7:38; 19:32,39.

[2]Luke uses it for the first time in Acts 5:11. This shows that it is only one of several terms he uses for the community of Christians.

[3]Luke uses the word ''covenant'' (*diatheke*) in Lk. 1:55,73; 22:20 (in some ancient manuscripts); Acts 3:25; 7:8.

[4]Chapter 4 is devoted entirely to Luke's understanding of the Hebrew scriptures.

[5]See Acts 2:41,47; 4:4; 5:14; 6:7; 9:42; 11:21,26; 14:1; 17:4; 18:8: 19:20; 21:20.

[6]Luke uses *presbuteros* also in Acts 11:30; 16:4; 21:18.

[7]See Acts 6:1,7; 9:1,19,26,38; 11:29; 13:52; 14:20,22,28; 15:10; 18:23; 19:1,9; 20:1,30; 21:4.

[8]See Acts 19:9:22:4; 24:14,22.

[9]Luke speaks of believing or those who believe in many texts: Acts 2:44; 4:32; 5:14; 6:7; 9:42; 11:21; 14:1; 15:5; 16:34; 17:12; 18:8; 19:18; 21:20.

[10]Note references in Chapter 1 to the many places in Acts where ''witness'' language is used.

[11]Three texts combine them: Acts 4:2; 15:35; 28:31.

[12]The noun for teaching (*didache*) occurs in Acts 5:28; 13:12; 17:19; the verb *didaskein* occurs some 16 times.

[13]The Greek verbs ''to preach'' are *kerussein* and *kataggellein*. See Acts 8:4-5; 9:20; 10:42; 13:5,38; 15:36; 16:17; 17:3,13,23; 26:23. For references to *euaggelizesthai*, ''to-preach-the-gospel,'' see Chapter 1.

[14]This text (Acts 16:16-40) combines the internal life and public witness of the church in an amazing way. On the one hand there is praying, singing, speaking the word, washing of wounds, baptizing, eating, rejoicing, believing. On

the other hand there is freeing a woman from personal and economic bondage; confronting the collusion of economic, political, police power; calling public officials to accountability. And it all takes place because of the persistency of a slave girl who would not be silent.

[15]See Acts 18:12-17; 21:27-32; 22:22-29; 23:12-24; 25:1-5.

CHAPTER 10

What You and I Want for the World

"Glory to God in the highest heaven, and on earth peace" (Lk. 1:14).

Bold and unhindered witness

I concluded my two-part story of Jesus and early Christians, *Luke-Acts*, with Paul in Rome. Though under arrest, he was free to proclaim God's reign and teach about the Lord Jesus Christ unhindered *with all boldness* (Acts 28:31). I used the same phrase in a prayer of Peter after his and John's release from prison, yet while still under threat. "And now, Lord, look at their threats, and grant to your servants to speak the word *with all boldness* (Acts 4:29).

I wanted to conclude *Acts* with such words ringing in the ears of my community and to encourage their bold witness. I wanted for that witness to be bold and unhindered by either religious or political threat. I didn't want the Christian witness crushed in my time because people saw us falsely as rabble-rousers and insurrectionists. I wanted for people, both inside and outside the church, to see that God's message in Jesus was a message of peace and "good news of great joy for all people."

Yes, it was a message to upset the whole world, to turn it upside down (Acts 17:6), not in terms of crushing, military might but of God's compassionate, merciful "peace by Jesus Christ" (Acts 10:36). It was a message to let God's gifts of empathy and embrace, love and liberty, justice and joy, health and wholeness unite the whole human family in an inclusive community.

Such a message called for witness "with all boldness" because the wellness of God's world was at stake. It is a boldness I wanted for me and my community in our continuing history.

A world without violence

As I tell the story, at the birth of Jesus, the heavenly host praised God and sang, "and on earth peace" (Lk. 2:14); and at his entrance into Jerusalem near the end of his peace ministry (note again Acts 10:36), a multitude of people praised God and said, "peace in heaven" (Lk. 19:38). God's moving toward us with peace in Jesus comes full circle with people responding and proclaiming peace toward God. That is what God intends.

Yet, almost immediately after the people proclaimed peace, Jesus wept over what he saw as the coming destruction of Jerusalem and said, "If you, even you, had only recognized on this day the things that make for peace" (Lk. 19:42). Since I wrote after that destruction, I knew what happened (see verses 43-44).

However, peace is more than the absence of conflict. With its roots in the Hebrew *shalom*, it is the presence of wholeness and health, harmony and well-being. It cannot embrace the violence that yields suffering, destruction, and death. In fact, violence erupts where there is no genuine peace, no wholeness of life.

We might think of Jesus' driving out the sellers in the temple as violent, but it had nothing to do with the violence that destroys human life (Lk. 19:45-46). It had to do with restoring what had become a den of robbers to its true purpose, a house of prayer. Pacifism is not passivism. Pacifism is "peace action" that seeks God's health in all of life's relationships.

I did not want the violence of Jerusalem's destruction to happen again in my time. Yet the history of the human race seems to be full of violence. Hebrew writers depict it in the story of Cain and Abel (Gen. 4:1-16). The story of Noah tells, "Now the earth was corrupt in God's sight, and the earth was filled with violence" (Gen. 6:12). World history, as well as Israel's history, knew so much violence and war.

Sometimes violence seems justified to free people from bondage (Israel's liberating exodus from Egypt was a violent act). Yet the destruction of one people by another leads to such feeling of revenge that it even creeps into a psalm: "Happy shall they be who take your little ones and dash them against a rock" (Ps. 137:9). Violence breeds violence.

Jesus anguished over violence.

> "Jerusalem, Jerusalem, the city that kills the prophets and stones those who are sent to it! How often have I desired to gather your children together as a hen gathers her brood under her wings, and you were not willing" (Lk. 13:34; note also the parable of the vineyard, Lk. 20:9-16).

Violence against Jesus himself led to his suffering and death (Lk. 22:63-23:49).

Yet God wove the worst that human beings can do toward God into the best that God can do for human beings (see Acts 2:23). Jesus' uncompromising obedience to God's loving and peaceful purpose at work in him goes all the way, even into death. It still is at work there as Jesus prays for his killers, pleading their ignorance: "Father, forgive them; for they do not know what they are doing" (Lk. 23:34; note also Acts 3:17; 17:30).

God can be present in and use human violence. I do not see God as causing or condoning it. Violence calls for "mind-changing" repentance, even when done in ignorance (Acts 3:17-19).

Acts tells of violence against the apostles and early Christians. Officials jailed Peter and John (Acts 4:1-3), jailed and beat the apostles (5:17-18,40), stoned Stephen to death (7:57-60), and persecuted the Church (8:1). Herod maltreated the church, killed the apostle James, and arrested Peter (12:1-3). Officials persecuted Paul and Barnabas (13:50), stoned Paul (14:19), beat and jailed Paul and Silas (16:22-24), beat and bound Paul with chains (21:30-32), and flogged and tied him with thongs (22:23-24). Had not the Roman tribune intervened, they would have ambushed and killed him (23:12-24).

I wanted all such violence to end! How senseless that the witnesses to "peace by Jesus Christ" should suffer such persecution, injury, death! I hoped that they would not reoccur in my time and that our witness to peace could go on "unhindered with all boldness" to "the ends of the earth" without violence. After all, our message was "good news of great joy for all the people."

But I feared that Jesus' words would still apply to us in my time: "If you, even you, had only recognized on this day the things that make for peace" (Lk. 19:42). Yet the witness to peace must go on. We simply had to say with Peter and John: "we cannot keep from speaking about what we have seen and heard" (Acts 4:20). I wonder whether we human beings just might be able one day to know a world without violence.

A world without walls

Jesus was born into a world full of walls: walls between heaven and earth, God and sinners, religious folk and despised outcasts; walls between Jews and Gentiles, Jews and Samaritans, Jerusalem and Rome; walls between healthy and sick, abled and disabled, poor and rich; walls between women and men, parents and children, slave and free; walls between nation states, language groups, social classes, religious traditions; walls between personal faith and public action, individual life and communal responsibility, time and eternity.

To read my story of Jesus is to see how God's Spirit at work in him broke through wall after wall to unite people, to include them at God's family table, to give them to one another as God's children, to ask them to care for one another, to invite them to repentance ("mind-change") and promise forgiveness ("letting go") and a new life with God, with one another, with the creation of "the God who made the world and everything in it" (Acts 17:24).

To read my story of the early church is to see how God's Spirit moves to break the barriers of language and gender and race, of relationship between Jews and Samaritans, Jews and Gentiles, Christians and Rome. The Christian witness moved across all the political boundaries of our known Mediterranean world: western Asia and northwest Africa, Greece and Italy, the islands of the sea. It showed the march of God's good news for all.

That march did meet resistance, but I wanted to show that God wants one human family in a world without walls.

A mutuality of women with men

I wanted a world where women are partners with men as witnesses to God's good news in Jesus. I wrote about this earlier, but here I want to spell it out in more detail. I see it as crucial that half the human race be neither subordinate to nor superior to men but partners together in faith and life and witness. I shall highlight the places where women appear in my writings.

In the Infancy Stories (Lk. 1:42-55) are the powerful witnesses of Elizabeth (John the Baptist's mother) and Mary (Jesus' mother) and the thanksgiving of the 84 year old prophet and widow, Anna (Lk. 2:36-38). Our Savior did come to us through a woman!

Jesus speaks of God's work beyond Israel and points to a widow at Zarephath in Sidon (Lk. 4:25-26). He heals Simon Peter's mother-in-law (4:38-39; Peter was married!). He raises a widow's son (7:11-17). He praises the love of a sinful woman (7:36-50).

Some women ("Mary, called Magdalene. . . Joanna. . . Susanna, and many others") join Jesus and the twelve in their mission and support them (8:1-3). Jesus' mother comes to him (8:19). Jesus restores the daughter of a synagogue leader, Jairus (8:40-42, 49-56) and heals and praises the faith of a hemorrhaging woman (8:43-48).

In a cultural setting that did not allow women to sit at the feet of a teacher, the story of Martha and Mary (10:38-42) lifts up Mary's sitting and listening to Jesus and promises that it "will not be taken away from her." There still were people in my time who wanted to maintain or restore old patterns.[1]

A woman blesses Jesus' mother (11:27). The "queen of the South" (the black queen of Sheba, 1 Kings 10:1-10), who came to listen to Solomon, will rise to judge those who do not see that (in Jesus) something greater than Solomon is here (11:31).

Jesus heals a woman crippled for eighteen years (13:10-17). He speaks a parable about a woman who seeks for a lost coin until she finds it (15:8-10), and another about a woman who is persistent in prayer (18:1-8). He tells of a poor widow who gave everything she had (21:1-4). A servant girl confronts Peter with the truth (22:56-57).

Women follow Jesus to the cross and wail for him. He says to them: "Daughters of Jerusalem, do not weep for me, but weep for yourselves and for your children" (23:27-28). Women stood at a distance watching Jesus' crucifixion (23:49) and go to the tomb, perplexed and terrified, but it is they who remember Jesus' words and who tell the apostles and others that Jesus has been raised (24:1-10; they are Mary Magdalene, Joanna, James' mother Mary, and other women).[2]

The numbers of women in *Luke* are impressive: twenty different individual women and four groups of women are part of my story. In my use of Mark's Gospel, I note that Mark has less than half that many individual women and only one group of women. In a culture that often devalued women and made them subservient to men, I wanted to move toward lifting them up as partners.

What about women in *Acts*? In the story of the early Christians after Jesus' resurrection, again I lift up their partnership.

Jesus' mother and other women join the apostles in prayerful waiting for the Spirit's empowerment (Acts 1:14). Peter refers to Joel's prophecy about the Spirit being poured out on Israel's daughters and God's slave women so they can prophesy (2:17-18).

Great is the number of both men and women believers (5:14). The apostles solve the needs of widows (6:1-4). Philip baptized both women and men (8:12). Saul persecutes both men and women disciples (9:1-2). Peter, surrounded by weeping widows, raises Tabitha (Dorcas) from death, a woman "devoted to good works and acts of charity" (9:36-42).

John Mark's mother Mary provides hospitality and Rhoda runs to tell of Peter's release from prison (12:12-14). Lydia opens her heart to Paul's message, is baptized, and provides hospitality (16:14-15,40). A slave girl points to Paul and Silas as proclaimers of salvation (16:17). Greek women and men of high standing believe (17:12) and a woman named Damaris and others became believers (17:34). Priscilla and Aquilla provide hospitality for Paul (18:1-3) and explain the Way of God more accurately to Apollos (18:26). The evangelist Philip's four unmarried daughters are prophets (21:8-9, those who "speak for" God).

Paul's sister's son warns of an ambush to kill Paul (23:16). Governor Felix's Jewish wife Drucilla sends for Paul and hears him speak of faith in Christ Jesus (24:24). King Agrippa's wife Bernice agrees with others that Paul has done nothing to deserve death or punishment (26:30-31).

Acts adds the names of ten different individual women and ten groups of women. Joined with the numbers in *Luke* makes for thirty individual women and fourteen groups of women. Though some, like men, are the recipients of ministry, many are active in some form of ministry, be it praise, prayer, prophecy (preaching), teaching, loving, caring, weeping, giving monetary support, providing hospitality, being the subject of exemplary parables.

In my writing, all this did not happen by chance. I did indeed want to lift up the partnership of women and men in ministry and the rich contribution of both in sharing/living God's good news.

A world without poverty

I lived in a world with great differences in wealth between the rich and the poor. Some had so much, others had almost nothing. Some lived in luxury in great mansions, others lived in poverty in shacks or even with "nowhere to lay their head" (Lk. 9:58). I wanted to see a world where such great disparity was gone, and I touch the matter of rich and poor a number of times. Let me now point to some of them.

In the Infancy Stories, Mary sings that God

"has brought down the powerful from their thrones, and lifted up the lowly;. . . filled the hungry with good things, and sent the rich away empty" (Lk. 1:52-53).

In the birth story, Mary laid Jesus in a manger, the feed-place of animals, "because there was no place for them in the inn" (Lk. 2:7); and the first persons to receive the "good news of great joy" were outcast shepherds (2:8-12).

John the Baptist's preaching links repentance to economics. "Whoever has two coats must share with anyone who has none; and whoever has food must do likewise" (3:11). He warned tax collectors to "collect no more than the amount prescribed for you (3:13) and soldiers to "not extort money from anyone by threats or false accusations" (3:14).

Jesus explains his mission with words from Isaiah, "The Spirit of the Lord is upon me, because he has anointed me to bring good news to the poor" (4:18; also 7:22), and he points to Elijah's help of a famine-stricken, destitute widow (4:25-26).

In his "sermon on the plain" Jesus turns to the Hebrew Scripture's pattern of pronouncing blessing and woe.

"Blessed are you who are poor, for yours is the kingdom of God. Blessed are you who are hungry now, for you will be filled" (6:20-21).

But woe to you who are rich, for you have received your consolation. Woe to you who are full now, for you will be hungry" (6:24-25).

Jesus goes on to say,

"If you lend to those from whom you hope to receive, what credit is that to you? For even sinners lend to sinners, to receive as much again. But love your enemies, do good, and lend, expecting nothing in return. Your reward will be great, and you will be children of the Most High; for he is kind to the ungrateful and the wicked. Be merciful as your Father is merciful" (6:34-36).

In Jesus' parable of showing mercy, the Good Samaritan not only gives "first aid" to the stripped, beaten, and half dead man, he provides for continuing care (10:34-35).

To the person who wanted him to settle an inheritance problem, Jesus replied, "Take care! Be on your guard against all kinds of greed; for one's life does not consist in the abundance of possessions" (12:15).

Jesus then proceeded to tell the parable of the rich fool who built bigger barns and said to himself, "Soul, you have ample goods laid up for many years; relax, eat, drink, be merry." But he died that night. "So it is with those who store up treasures for themselves but are not rich toward God" (12:16-21; a message of God's caring for human needs follows, 12:22-31).

As to luncheon or dinner parties, Jesus calls not for inviting friends or relatives or rich neighbors, but "invite the poor, the crippled, the lame, and the blind. . . because they cannot repay you" (14:12-14; note also vs. 21).

He tells the story of the rich man, finely dressed and eating sumptuously, and the poor Lazarus, covered with sores and longing for the crumbs from the rich man's table (16:19-31). Both die, the rich man tormented in Hades (place of the dead) and Lazarus with Abraham. It pictures Jesus' earlier teaching about blessing and woe (6:20-21,24-25).[3]

Further is the story of the ruler, a commandment-keeping good man, but whose life's center was his wealth (18:18-23). Jesus called him to "Sell all that you own and distribute the money to the poor, and you will have treasure in heaven; then come, follow me." Hearing this, the man "became sad; for he was very rich."

Jesus comments,

"How hard it is for those who have wealth to enter the kingdom of God! Indeed, it is easier for a camel to go through the eye of a needle than for someone who is rich to enter the kingdom of God" (18:24-25).

Some asked him, "Then who can be saved?" Jesus replied, "What is impossible for mortals is possible for God" (18:26-27). And it was possible for the rich tax collector Zacchaeus. God's encounter with Zacchaeus in Jesus made it possible for him to become an honest tax collector, who quadrupled his payback for fraud and gave half his goods to the poor (19:1-10).

Finally in *Luke* I contrast rich people and a poor widow. They gave "out of their abundance;" she "out of her poverty" gave "all she had to live on" (21:1-4).

Jesus confronts us with the matter of the rich and the poor many times to show that the use of this world's goods is crucial in following him. Jesus calls us to treasure, not material goods but God's reign of compassion. Then our use of goods will have their proper place in furthering that reign. Jesus said, "For where your treasure is, there your heart will be also" (12:32).

In *Acts* I tell also of economic concerns. The two texts below point to how early Christians tried to meet material needs.

> "And all who believed were together and had all things in common; they would sell their possessions and goods and distribute the proceeds to all, as any had need. Day by day, as they spent much time together in the temple, they broke bread at home and ate their food with glad and generous hearts, praising God and having the goodwill of all the people" (Acts 2:44-47).

> "Now the whole group of those who believed were of one heart and soul, and no one claimed private ownership of any possessions, but everything they owned was in common. With great power the apostles gave their testimony to the resurrection of the Lord Jesus, and great grace was upon them all. There was not a needy person among them, for as many as owned lands or houses sold and brought the proceeds of what was sold. They laid it at the apostles' feet, and it was distributed to each as any had need" (4:32-35).

Dishonesty did create problems for such a system (see 5:1-11).

In Jerusalem they worked out a plan to meet the needs of a group of neglected widows (6:1-4); and in Antioch, anticipating a severe famine, the disciples "determined that according to their ability, each would send relief to the believers living in Judea; this they did, sending it to the elders by Barnabas and Saul'' (11:27-29).

Tabitha ''was devoted to good works and acts of charity'' (9:6). Lydia provided hospitality for Paul and Silas (16:14-15), as did the Philippian jailer (16:34). When Paul was in jail in Caesarea, the governor allowed Paul's friends to care for his needs (24:23).

On the way to Rome, when they put into port at Sidon, the Roman centurion kindly allowed Paul to go to his friends to receive care (27:3), and later Paul showed concern for hungry sailors:

"he took bread; and giving thanks to God in the presence of all, he broke
it and began to eat. Then all of them were encouraged and took food for
themselves'' (27:36).

I tell all these instances in my writings to show that concern for meeting material needs is an essential part of the total picture of both Jesus and the early Christians. In light of Jesus' teaching, as well as of the Hebrew prophets, distributing wealth justly needs to be a major concern. Jesus points to the sorry destiny of those who revel in luxury when others are destitute (Lk. 16:19-31).

Jesus brought good news to the poor and blessed them. This was not to keep them poor but to lift them up as those with hands open to God's reign and God's gifts. With hands closed around their wealth, the rich cannot know God's reign until they release their grasp and let their wealth flow to meet the needs of the poor. I wanted a world where all human needs are met.

Unity with diversity

Unity does not mean uniformity. Our confession that Jesus Christ is Lord united all of us early Christians. Our relationship to him and to the God at work in him united us. Yet when we began to live and think and speak about Jesus in our various contexts and congregations, there was room for much diversity. Our Hebrew Scriptures themselves were full of diversity.

I think about our diverse witness as part of the ongoing, interpretive work of the Holy Spirit. The Spirit is at work to make the message of good news alive in each particular place. As I look back upon them now, each gospel writer wrote and adapted the good news to a particular time and place.

I knew Mark's Gospel, but it just would not do for me simply to repeat Mark and other writers; their audiences were not mine. I needed to reshape my materials in imaginative ways that would speak to my community and meet its needs. I see that creative shaping and reshaping as one way the Spirit is at work.

This means that diversity will arise among us, a diversity that can enrich our unity and help us see that we cannot box Jesus Christ into one simple package to fit every situation. We will have different ways of speaking about God, Jesus, the Holy Spirit, baptism, the Lord's Supper, history, salvation. That diversity need not divide but enrich us as we appreciate and listen and learn from one another. We can debate vigorously and differ from one another, but we dare not break the unity nor fail to care for one another.

A problem arises when any one person or group thinks that they alone have the right theology, the right "understanding of God." Or that they have the right understanding of scripture. Sometimes people create what they regard as the right doctrine *about* the Bible. The danger then is that we make the Bible fit the doctrine we have made.

To do this is no longer to let the Bible be what it is, with all the rough edges and diversity that quite naturally have come from a thousand years of writing in many different settings and to meet many different situations. It forces a unity that means uniformity, rather than allowing for the rich diversity that arises from all the give and take, faithfulness and faithlessness, of our human encounter with God and one another.

As we interpret scripture in community, there is room for a rich diversity of interpretation. In my time, we certainly did interpret our Hebrew scriptures in different ways. What is important is that our interpretation *build* persons, not tear them down; *build* community, not disrupt it; *build* the peace of God's gift to us in Jesus Christ.

To shake another's hand creates a unity between persons. To talk about the handshake will bring diverse comments, none of which can ever be a substitute for the handshake itself. Theology is our diverse talk about God, but our unity is in God's handshake with us in Jesus Christ. That handshake is "good news of great joy for all the people."

Endnotes

[1]We can see this within the New Testament itself in texts like 1 Tim. 2:8-15. Though written in Paul's name, most scholars regard it as written in Paul's name in the second generation after Paul's death about the turn of the first century.

[2]The lists of women differ in each of the four gospels, though they have some names in common.

[3]I have dealt with only one aspect of this text. The entire story has other important points to make.

For Further Study

Aland, K. (editor), *Synopsis of the Four Gospels*. Revised English Edition, New York: United Bible Societies, 1985. This provides a valuable tool for comparing the gospels and discerning their similarities, differences, and the various emphases of each.

Achtemeier, P.J. (editor), *The Harper Bible Dictionary*, San Francisco: Harper & Row, 1985. Another valuable tool in understanding names, words, places, and themes.

Craddock, F.B., *Luke*. Interpretation, A Bible Commentary for Teaching and Preaching, Louisville: John Knox Press, 1990. An excellent, exciting, and very readable commentary.

Fitzmyer, J., *The Gospel According to Luke I-IX* and *The Gospel according to Luke X-XXIV*. Anchor Bible. Garden City, NY: Doubleday, 1981, 1985. This two volume commentary is a classic for detailed study of introductory concerns, the text, and theological understanding.

Kohlenberger, J. III, *New Revised Standard Concordance Unabridged*, Grand Rapids: Zondervan Publishing House, 1991. The use of a concordance leads one to the places where a biblical writers use particular words. This lets the biblical writer help the interpreter understand the ways in which a writer like Luke's use of words in various places illuminates the use in a text under study.

Powell, M.A., *What are they saying about Luke?*, New York/Mahwah: Paulist Press, 1989. A very readable and fine overview of scholarly issues with an excellent bibliography of the scholars involved.

Powell, M. A., *What are they saying about Acts?*, New York/Mahwah: Paulist Press, 1991. The comments above on Luke hold for Acts as well.

Talbert, C. H., *Reading Luke:* A Literary and Theological Commentary on the Third Gospel. New York: Crossroad, 1986. An excellent presentation by a premier Lucan scholar.

Willimon, W.H., *Acts*. Interpretation, A Bible Commentary for Teaching and Preaching, Atlanta: John Knox Press, 1988. A lively and useful commentary on the second half of Luke's two-part work.

Selected Name and Subject Index